GO TO SLEEP (I MISS YOU)

LUCY KNISLEY

GO TO SLEEP (I MISS YOU)

Cartoons from the Fog of New Parenthood

First Second
New York

For Pal

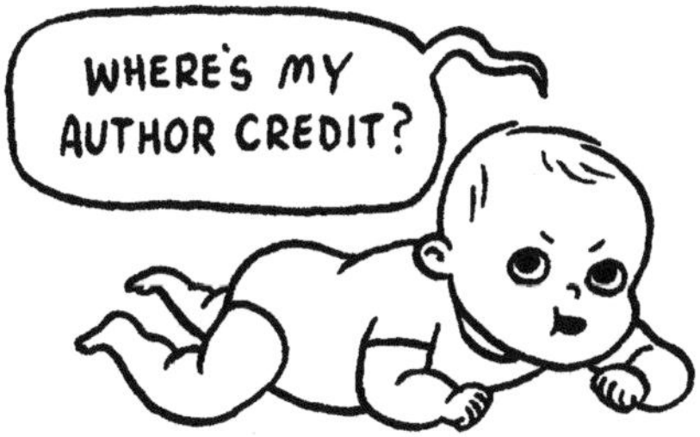
WHERE'S MY AUTHOR CREDIT?

CONTENTS

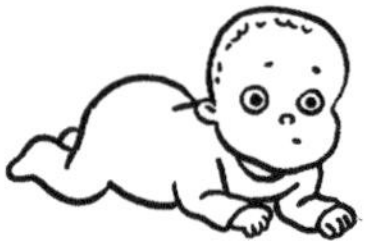

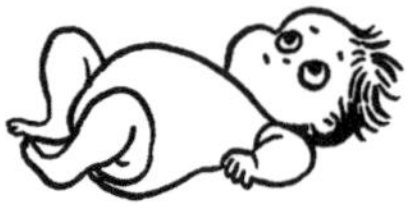

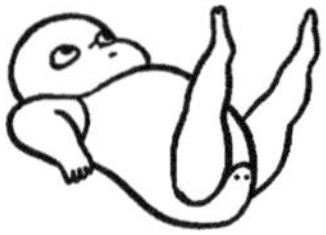

"Every baby born into the world
is a finer one than the last."
—Charles Dickens

"But seriously, though. Mine is the best."
—Me

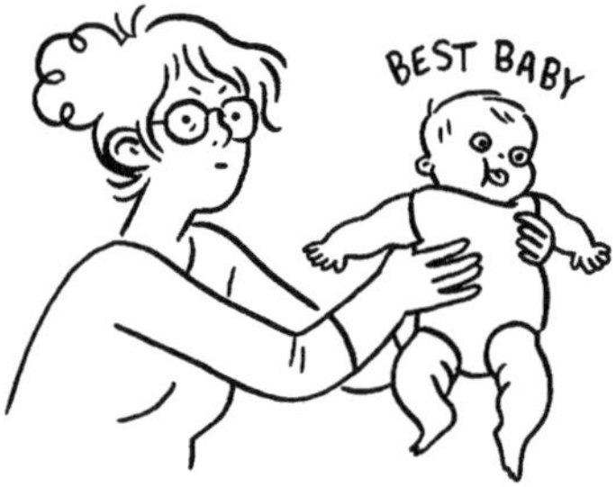
BEST BABY

Introduction from the Author

I spent much of my pregnancy worried that having a baby would derail my work. My *important* comic-book work.

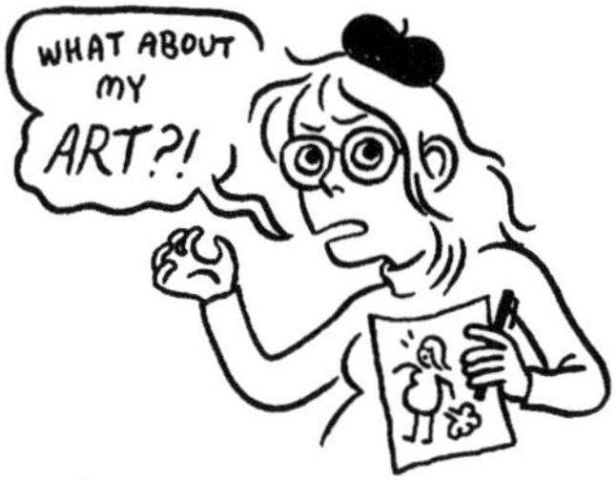
WHAT ABOUT MY ART?!

I was right. Having a baby derailed my work, my brain, my body, and the whole damn train.

I was on a new train, and that train was a Baby Express to Babyville.

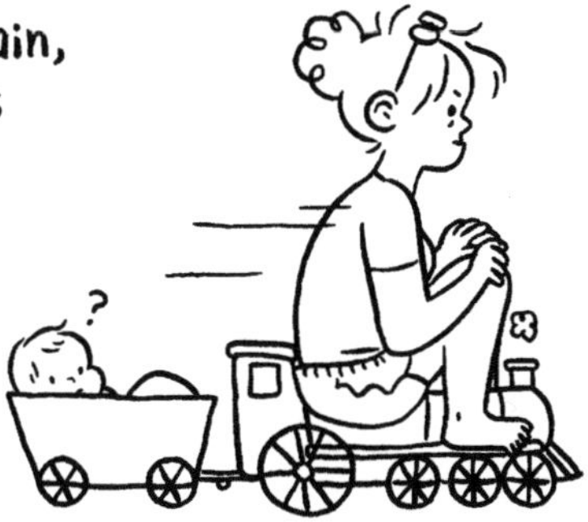
?

I've always kept sketchbooks. From my teen years on, the pages are filled with self-conscious agonies, embarrassing anecdotes, and indulgent why-me's.

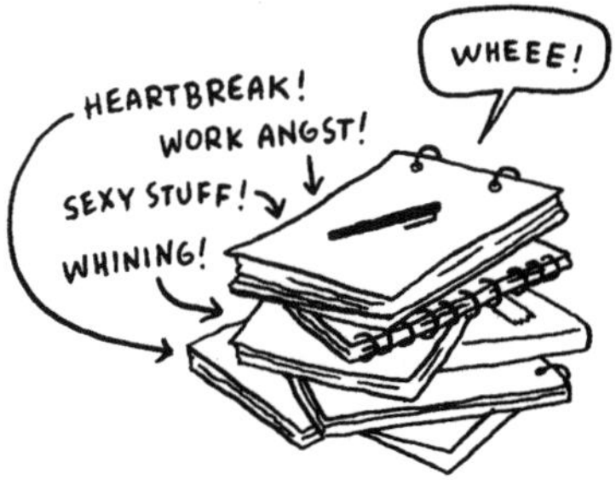
HEARTBREAK!
WORK ANGST!
SEXY STUFF!
WHINING!
WHEEE!

But as soon as I pulled myself out of the milk-sodden epidural haze enough to put down my baby for a minute and pick up a pen, my sketchbook became a hand-drawn baby book. Having previously used drawing as a way to understand the world, I was now using it to discover a completely new world and person and way of life—all of which felt at once bafflingly foreign and very sweet.

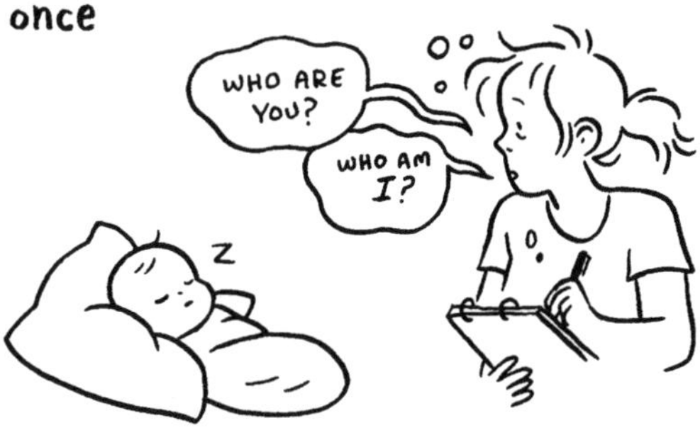
WHO ARE YOU?
WHO AM I?
Z

And hilarious, though that might have been the sleep deprivation.

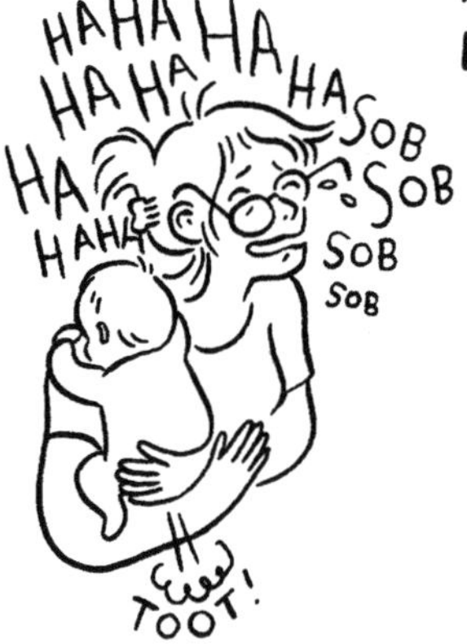
HAHA HA
HA HA HA
HA
HA
HAHA
HAHA
SOB
SOB
SOB
SOB
TOOT!

Looking back, I'm so glad I jotted down some thoughts on those days with a newborn. What a time to be alive, or to be born.

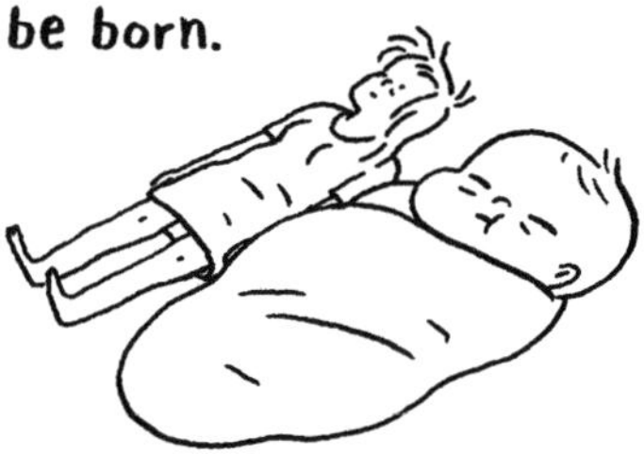

These little sketchbook cartoons are my effort to feel less alone and crazy at a time when most people feel alone and crazy.

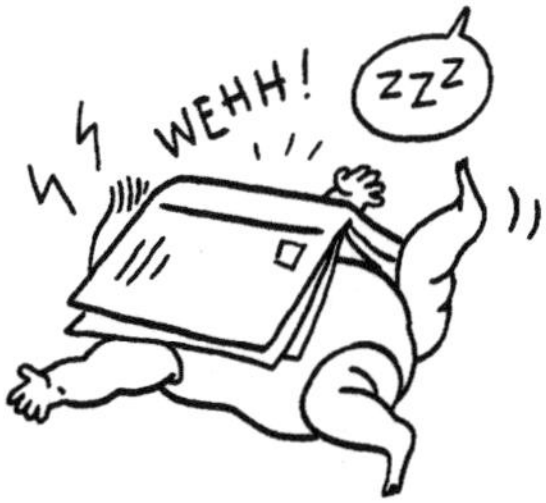
WEHH!
ZZZ

I hope they keep you company during late-night feeds. Don't fall asleep reading and drop the book on the baby, because then I'll feel bad, and you'll be able to blame me for being cranky in the morning.

Or, wait,
never mind—
blame me all
you want!

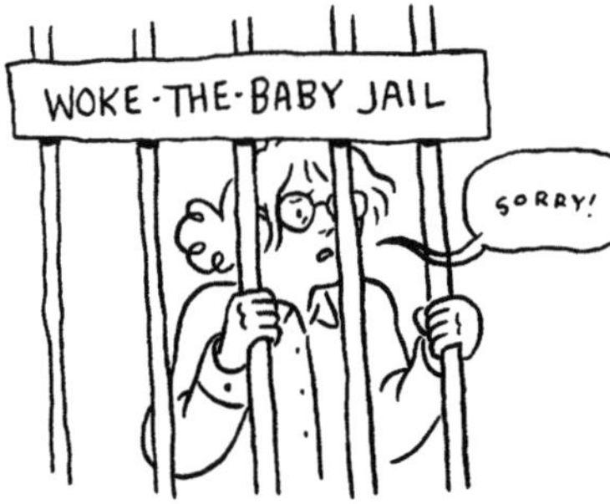
WOKE-THE-BABY JAIL
SORRY!

I'm happy to take on anything that helps.

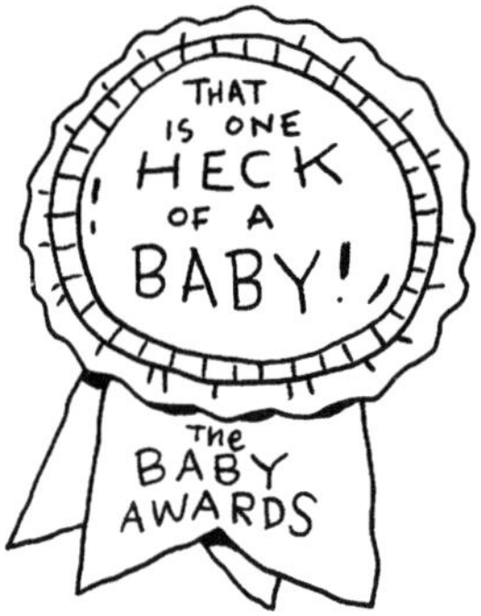
THAT IS ONE HECK OF A BABY!
THE BABY AWARDS

Good luck with your baby—

it's even finer than the last!

(Except for mine.)

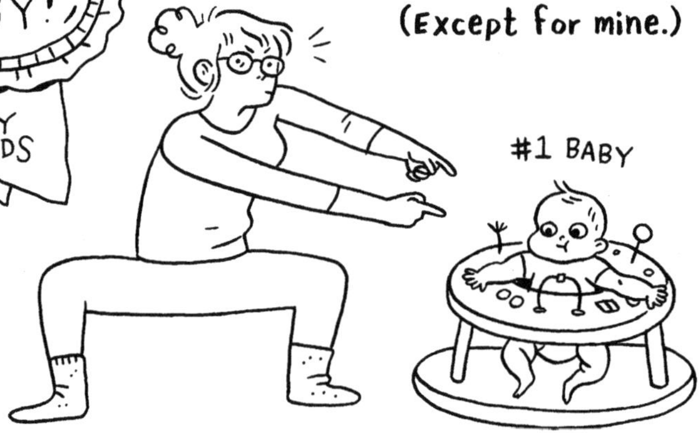
#1 BABY

GO TO SLEEP (I MISS YOU)

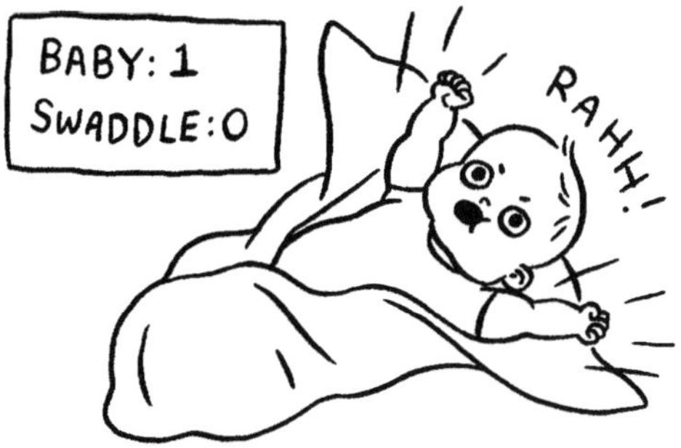
BABY: 1
SWADDLE: 0
RAHH!

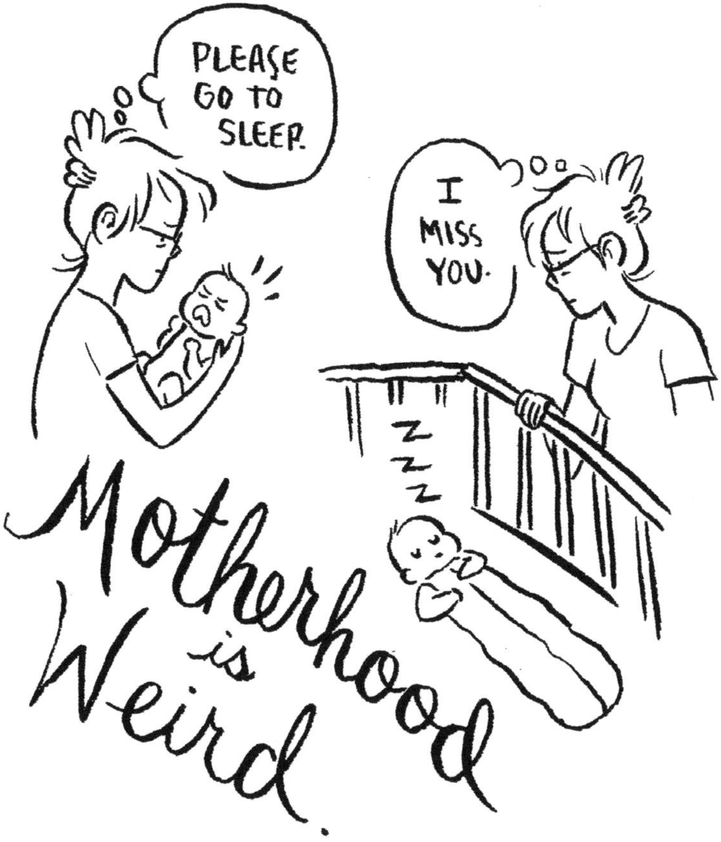
PLEASE GO TO SLEEP.
I MISS YOU.
Z Z Z
Motherhood is Weird.

After the baby goes to bed, we look at pictures of him.

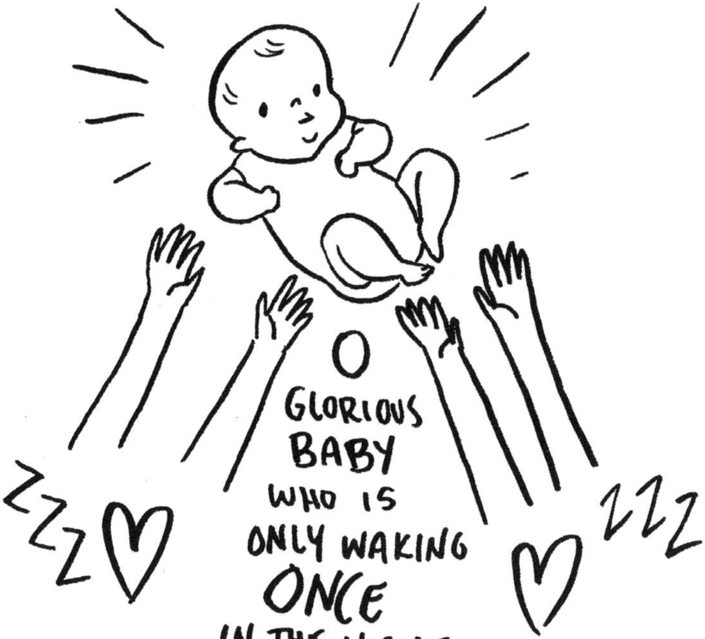

O
GLORIOUS
BABY
WHO IS
ONLY WAKING
ONCE
IN THE NIGHT,
CONTINUE TO GRANT US
THIS PEACE!

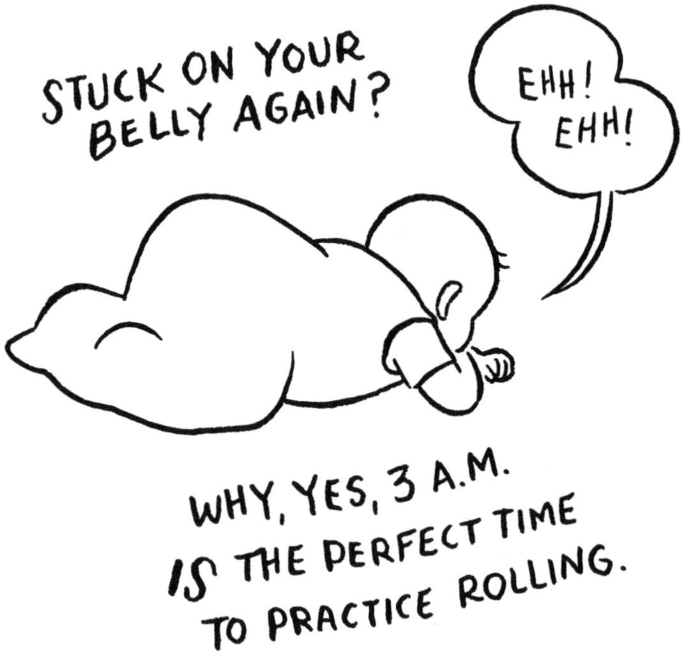
STUCK ON YOUR BELLY AGAIN?
EHH! EHH!
WHY, YES, 3 A.M. IS THE PERFECT TIME TO PRACTICE ROLLING.

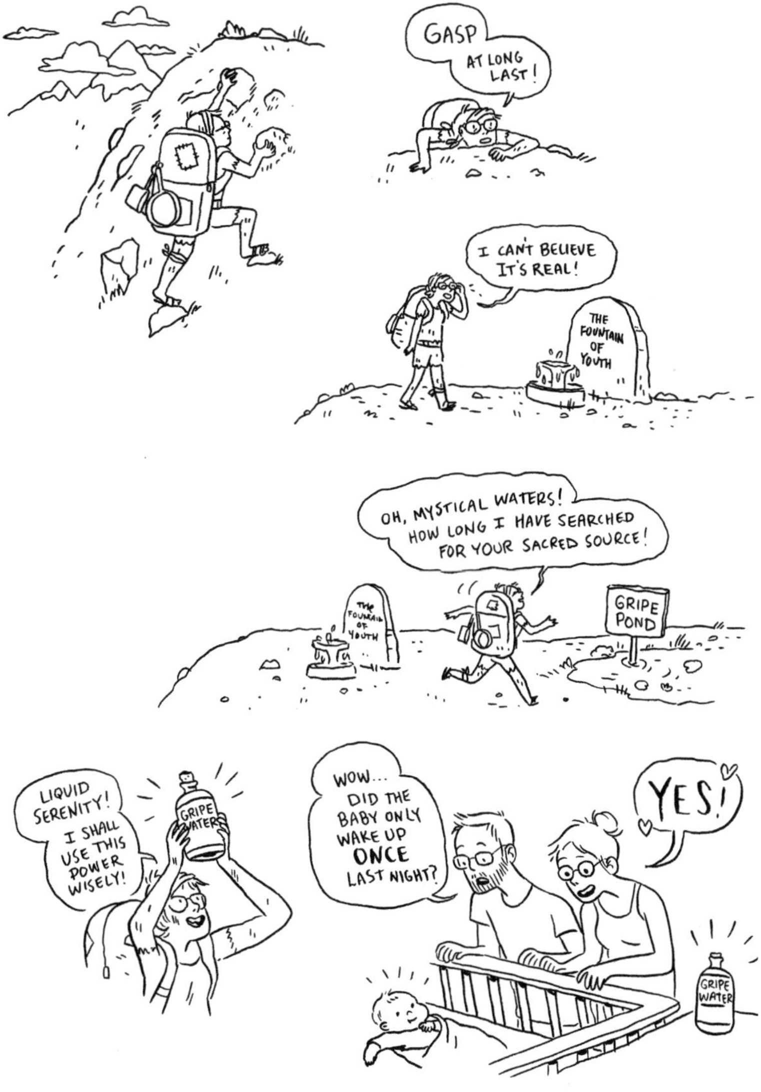
GASP
AT LONG LAST!
I CAN'T BELIEVE IT'S REAL!
THE FOUNTAIN OF YOUTH
OH, MYSTICAL WATERS! HOW LONG I HAVE SEARCHED FOR YOUR SACRED SOURCE!
THE FOUNTAIN OF YOUTH
GRIPE POND
LIQUID SERENITY!
I SHALL USE THIS POWER WISELY!
GRIPE WATER
WOW... DID THE BABY ONLY WAKE UP ONCE LAST NIGHT?
YES!
GRIPE WATER

-THE-
GLORIOUS
NAPCLOUD

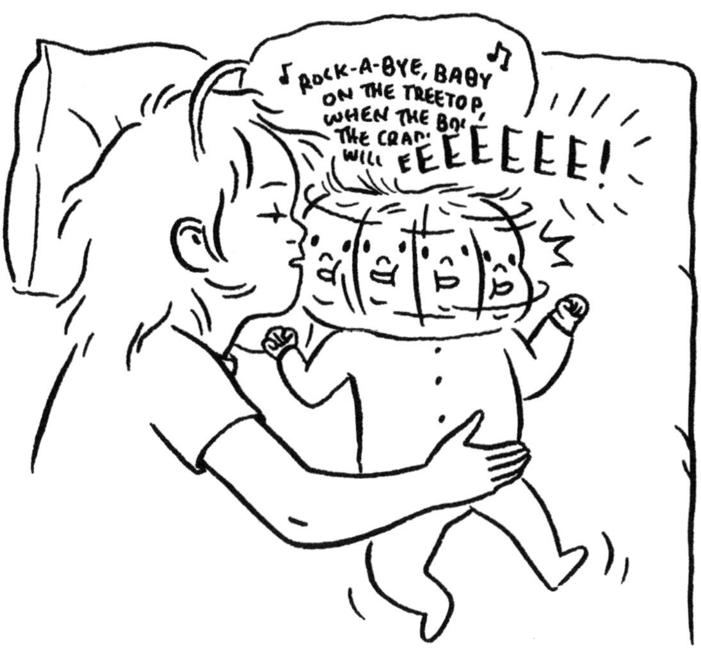
ROCK-A-BYE, BABY
ON THE TREETOP,
WHEN THE BO
THE CRA
WILL EEEEEEE!

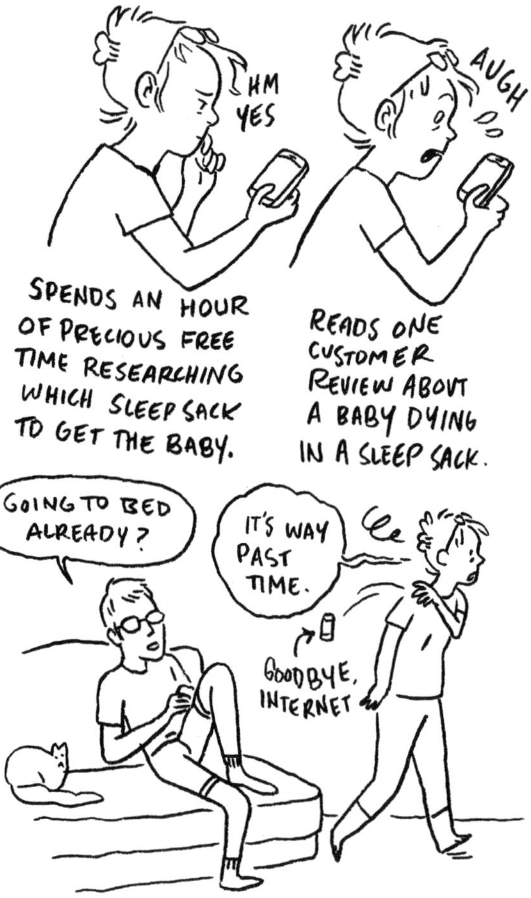
HM YES
AUGH
SPENDS AN HOUR OF PRECIOUS FREE TIME RESEARCHING WHICH SLEEP SACK TO GET THE BABY.
READS ONE CUSTOMER REVIEW ABOUT A BABY DYING IN A SLEEP SACK.
GOING TO BED ALREADY?
IT'S WAY PAST TIME.
GOODBYE, INTERNET

A
SOOTHING
SLEEP THRASH

CRIB WRIGGLE

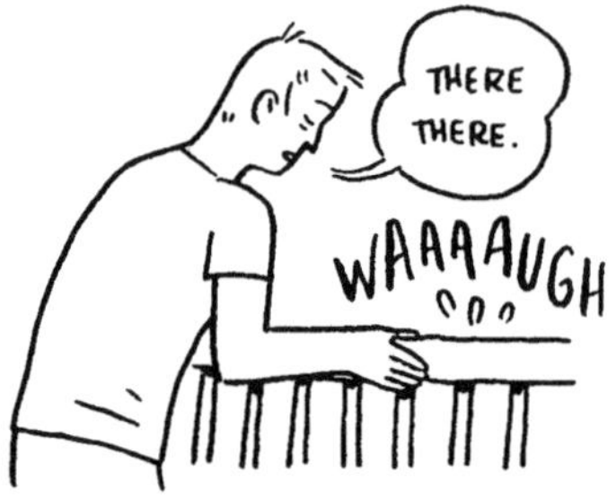
THERE THERE.
WAAAAUGH

JOHN'S VERSION OF
"ENCOURAGING THE BABY
TO SETTLE DOWN IN THE CRIB
WITHOUT NEEDING TO BE PICKED UP"

& MY VERSION →

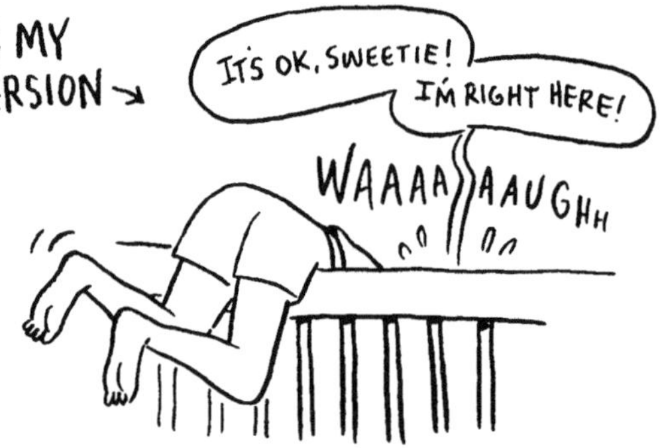
IT'S OK, SWEETIE!
I'M RIGHT HERE!
WAAAAAAAUGHH

SOMETIMES:

OTHER TIMES:

PAL SEEMS TO BE GOING THROUGH A SLEEP REGRESSION.
EHHHHH!
I'M AT A LEVEL OF EXHAUSTION...
YEEEHH!
AAAAA!
...WHERE IT SEEMS TO BE...
...AFFECTING MY DRAWING.
AAAAAAA

HE'S DRIFTING OFF!
TIME TO PUT HIM IN THE CRIB.
HUH?
SWING
OH WELL, GUESS I'M A MATTRESS NOW.

CHOW TIME

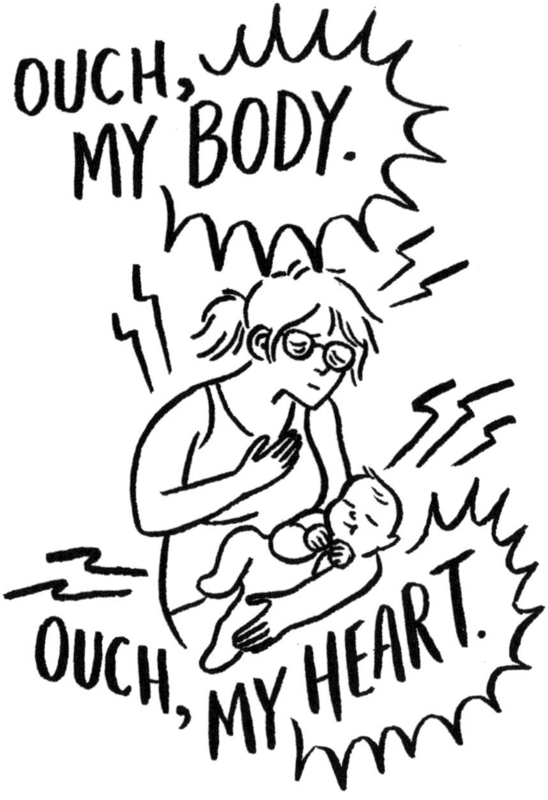
OUCH, MY BODY.
OUCH, MY HEART.

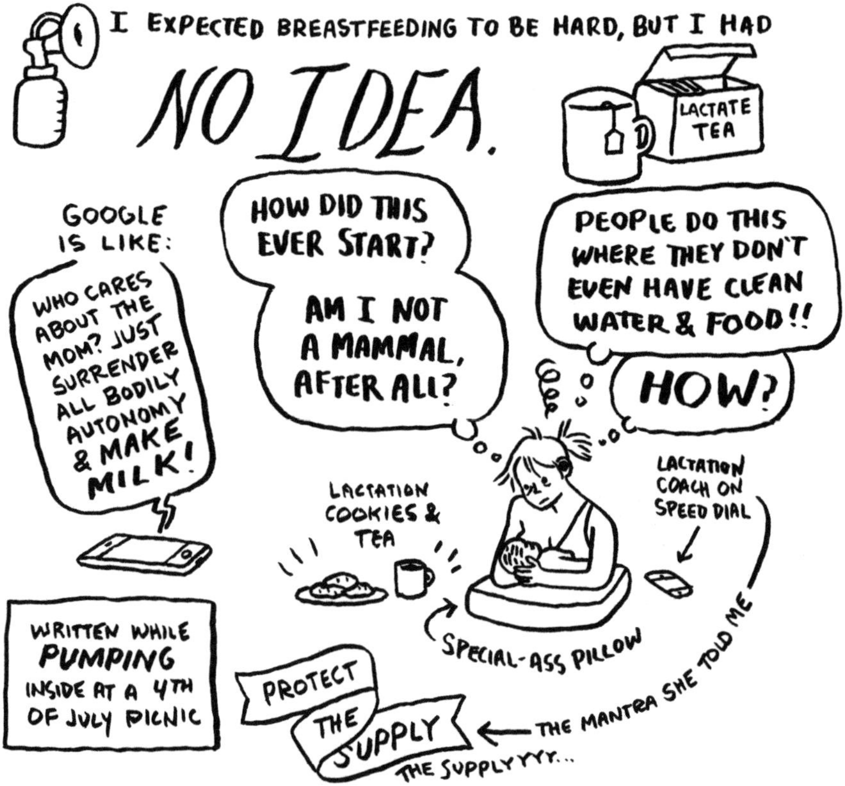

I EXPECTED BREASTFEEDING TO BE HARD, BUT I HAD
NO IDEA.
LACTATE TEA
GOOGLE IS LIKE:
WHO CARES ABOUT THE MOM? JUST SURRENDER ALL BODILY AUTONOMY & MAKE MILK!
HOW DID THIS EVER START?
AM I NOT A MAMMAL, AFTER ALL?
PEOPLE DO THIS WHERE THEY DON'T EVEN HAVE CLEAN WATER & FOOD!!
HOW?
LACTATION COOKIES & TEA
LACTATION COACH ON SPEED DIAL
SPECIAL-ASS PILLOW
WRITTEN WHILE PUMPING INSIDE AT A 4TH OF JULY PICNIC
PROTECT THE SUPPLY
THE SUPPLYYYY...
THE MANTRA SHE TOLD ME

I'VE BEEN CALLING THIS MOVE **THE MILKICK!**

IT DOES **NOT** LOOK COMFORTABLE, BUT **PAL IS VERY INTO IT** LATELY.

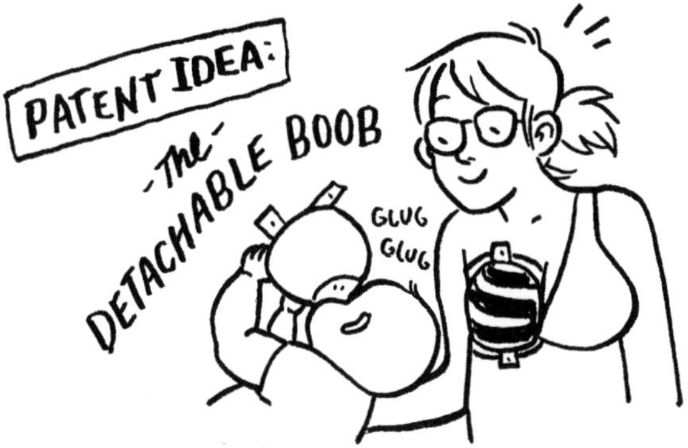
PATENT IDEA:
-The-
DETACHABLE BOOB
GLUG
GLUG

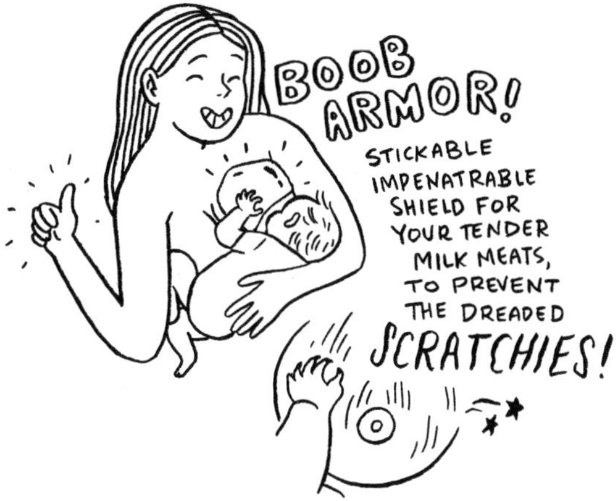
BOOB ARMOR!
STICKABLE IMPENATRABLE SHIELD FOR YOUR TENDER MILK MEATS, TO PREVENT THE DREADED
SCRATCHIES!

An UNEXPECTED Aspect of NEW MOTHERHOOD:

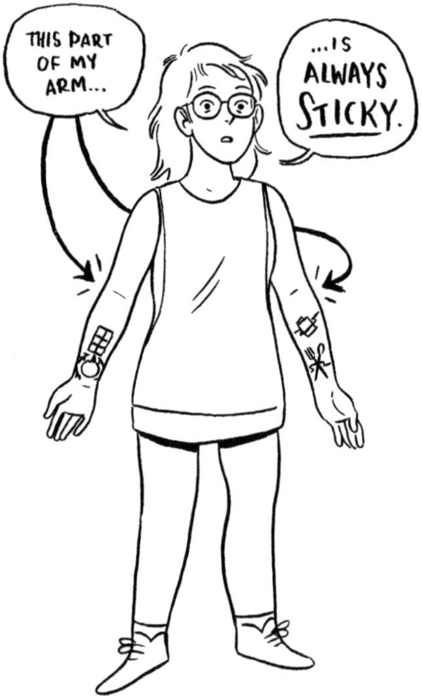
THIS PART OF MY ARM...
...IS ALWAYS STICKY.

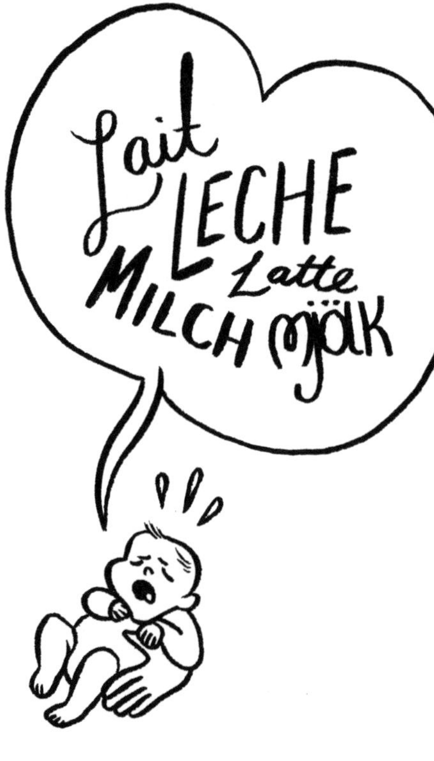
Lait
LECHE
Latte
MILCH
mjölk

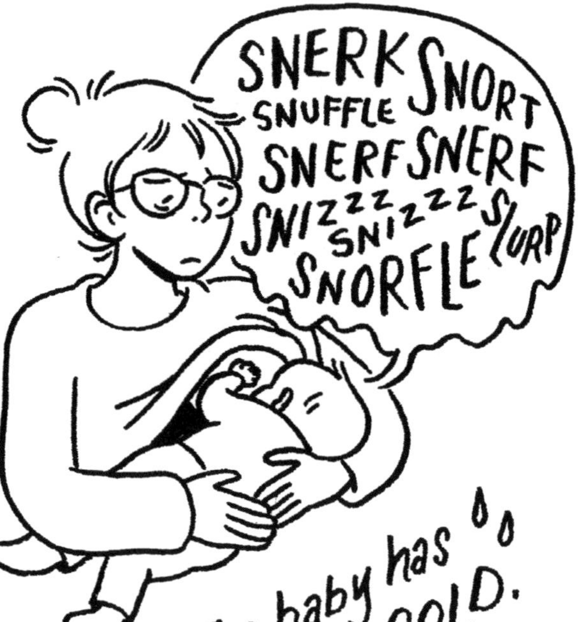
SNERK SNORT
SNUFFLE
SNERF SNERF
SNIZZZ SNIZZZ SLURP
SNORFLE

The baby has A LITTLE COLD.

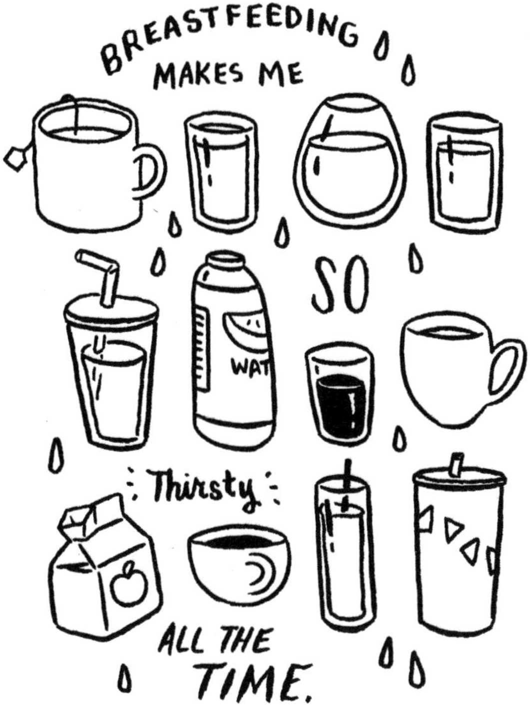
BREASTFEEDING
MAKES ME
SO
Thirsty
ALL THE
TIME.
WAT

LOOK, I WORK HARD

TO MAKE MILK
FOR YOU

SO I'D APPRECIATE IT

NO!!

IF YOU WOULD STOP
EATING WOODCHIPS
AT THE PARK!

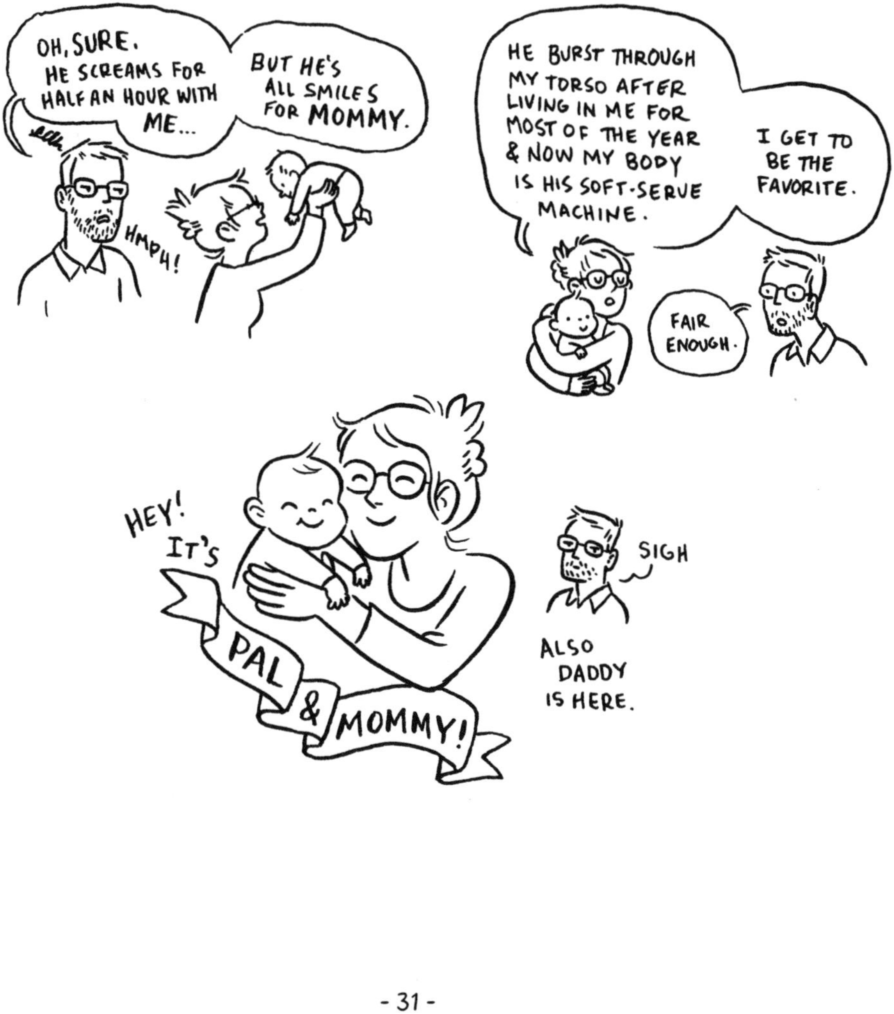
OH, SURE. HE SCREAMS FOR HALF AN HOUR WITH ME...
BUT HE'S ALL SMILES FOR MOMMY.
HMPH!
HE BURST THROUGH MY TORSO AFTER LIVING IN ME FOR MOST OF THE YEAR & NOW MY BODY IS HIS SOFT-SERVE MACHINE.
I GET TO BE THE FAVORITE.
FAIR ENOUGH.
HEY! IT'S
PAL & MOMMY!
SIGH
ALSO DADDY IS HERE.

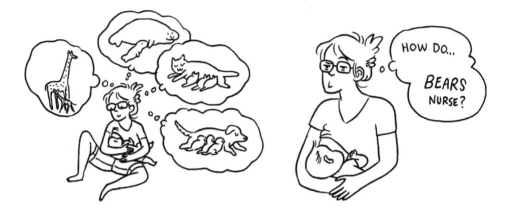

HOW DO... BEARS NURSE?

THE REASON SMART PHONES WERE INVENTED

BEAR NURSE?

IT TURNS OUT:

PRETTY MUCH LIKE HUMANS.

WHAT.

HEY, WHY IS OUR INTERNET SO SLOW?

I'M WATCHING THIS BEAR TITTY VIDEO.

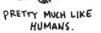

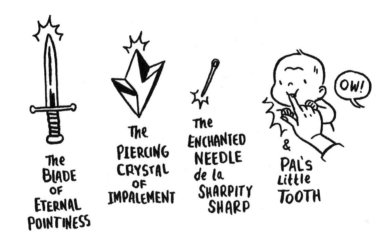

The
BLADE
OF
ETERNAL
POINTINESS

The
PIERCING
CRYSTAL
OF
IMPALEMENT

The
ENCHANTED
NEEDLE
de la
SHARPITY
SHARP

&
PAL'S
Little
TOOTH

OW!

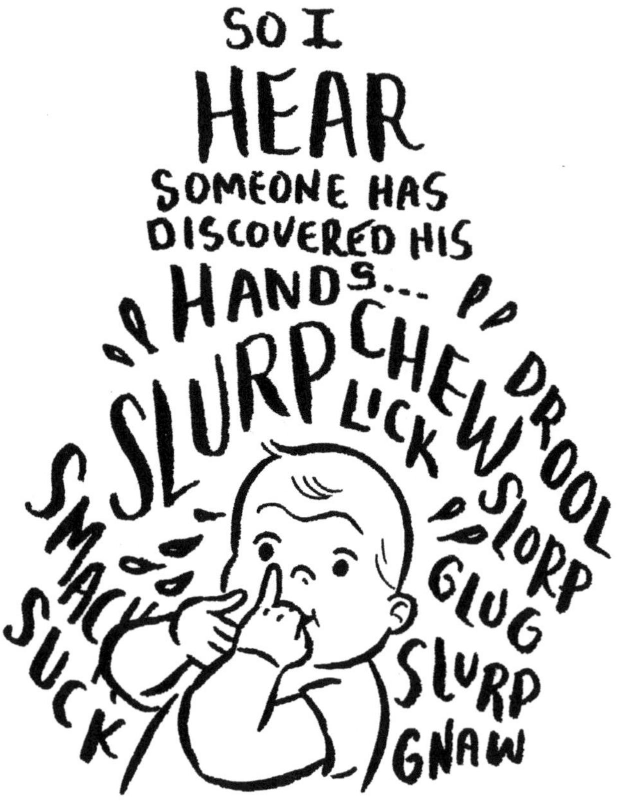
SO I HEAR SOMEONE HAS DISCOVERED HIS HANDS...
SLURP
CHEW
LICK
DROOL
SLORP
GLUG
SLURP
GNAW
SMACK
SUCK

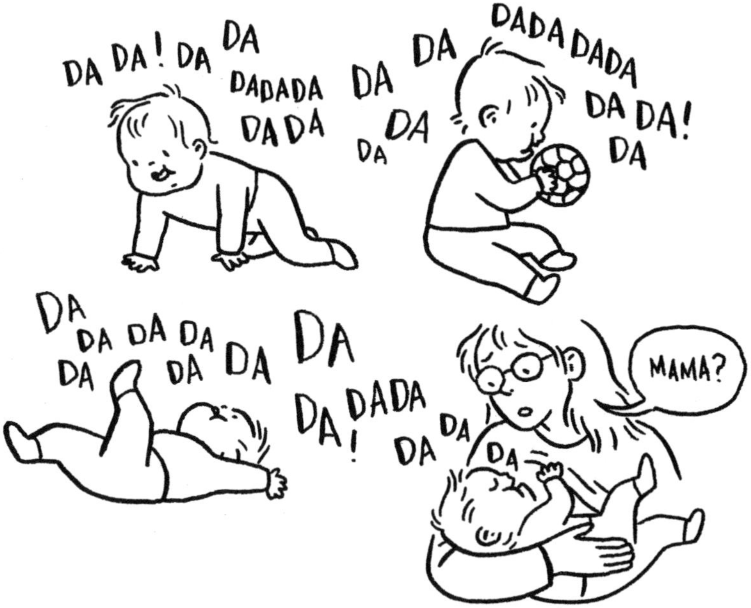
DA DA! DA DA
DADADA
DADA
DA DA
DADADADADA
DA DA! DA
DA DA DA DA DA DA DA DA DA DA
DA DADA DA!
DA DA DA
MAMA?

SUMMERTIME NURSING

·STICKY·SWEATY·HOT·MOIST·

AUTUMN NURSING

·SNUGGLY·COZY·HYGGE·WARM·

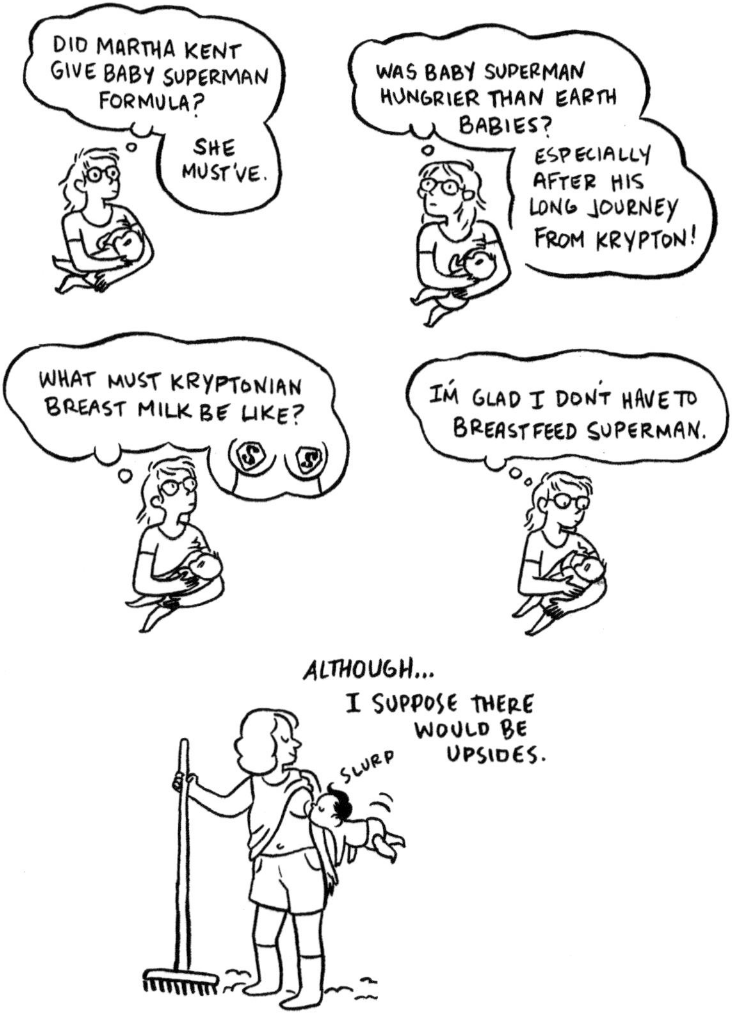
DID MARTHA KENT GIVE BABY SUPERMAN FORMULA?
SHE MUST'VE.
WAS BABY SUPERMAN HUNGRIER THAN EARTH BABIES?
ESPECIALLY AFTER HIS LONG JOURNEY FROM KRYPTON!
WHAT MUST KRYPTONIAN BREAST MILK BE LIKE?
I'M GLAD I DON'T HAVE TO BREASTFEED SUPERMAN.
ALTHOUGH...
I SUPPOSE THERE WOULD BE UPSIDES.
SLURP

Please oh PLEASE let someone say something.

I LOVE YOUR NOISY LITTLE MILK BREATHS.

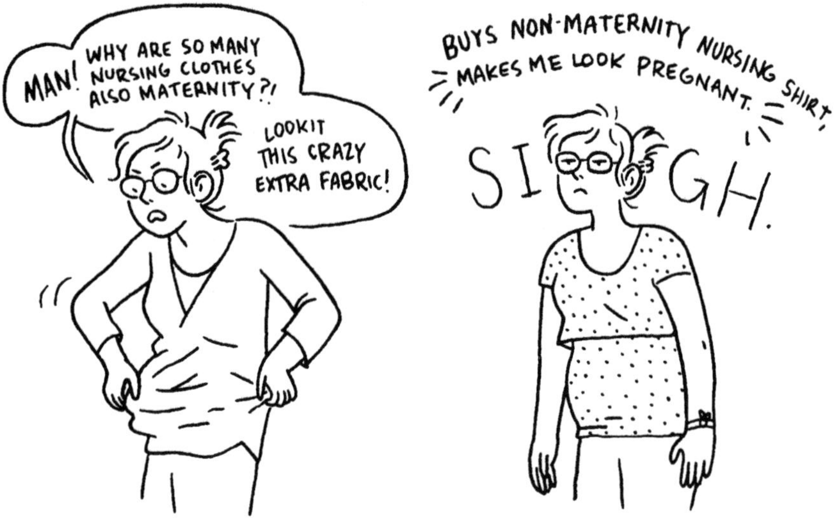
MAN! WHY ARE SO MANY NURSING CLOTHES ALSO MATERNITY?!
LOOKIT THIS CRAZY EXTRA FABRIC!
BUYS NON-MATERNITY NURSING SHIRT, MAKES ME LOOK PREGNANT.
SIGH.

YA HUNGRY, SWEETIE?
HA HA, OKAY, HERE YA GO!
GASP
GLOM
GOOD?

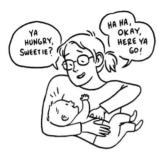

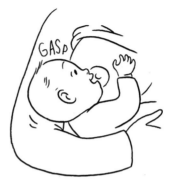

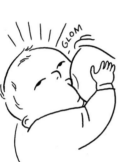

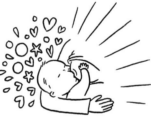

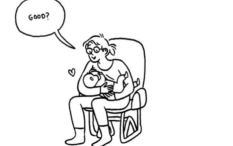

JUICE MILK TEA KEFIR

YOG

OATMEAL
W/ FRUIT

EGG IN A
HOLE

REMEMBER
BEFORE BREASTFEEDING
WHEN I COULD
SKIP
BREAKFAST?
All this
GETS ME TO
ELEVEN.

COGNITIVE DISSONANCE
I love you
you're my world
HOW
CHOMP
DARE YOU?!

CHOMP
CHOMP
SCRATCH
SCRATCH

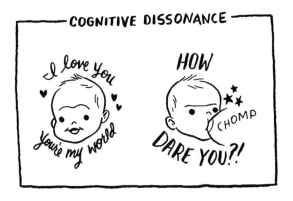

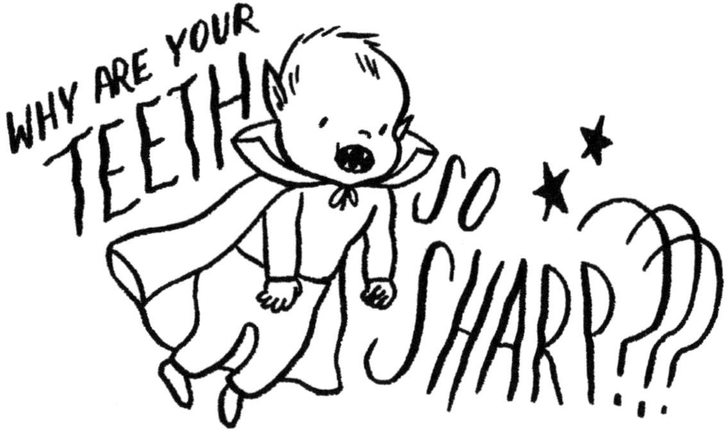
WHY ARE YOUR
TEETH
SO
SHARP???...

PAL HAS TWO TEETH, & BREAST-FEEDING **HURTS** _BAD,_ BUT I STILL DO IT.

KITTENS HAVE **TONS** OF TINY NEEDLE TEETH! MAMA CATS ARE **BADASS!**

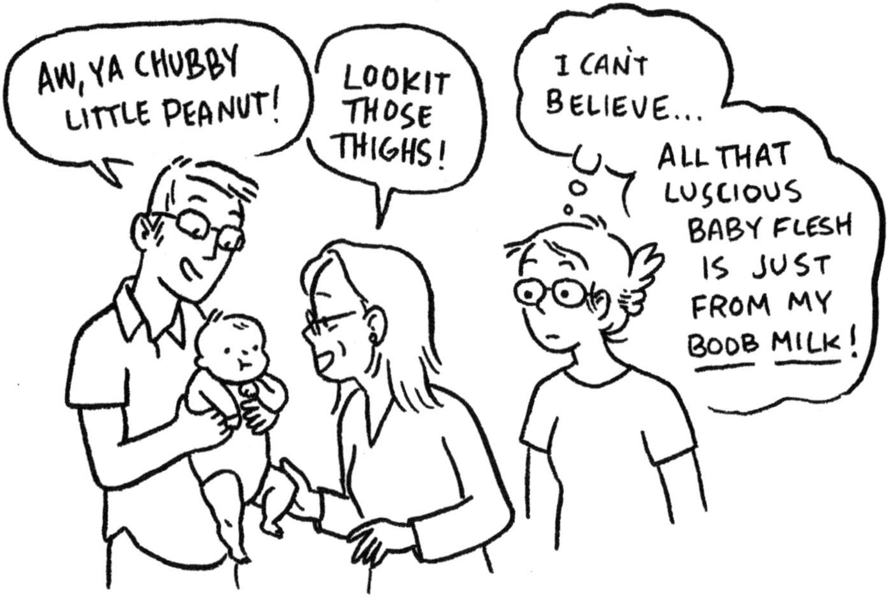
AW, YA CHUBBY LITTLE PEANUT!
LOOKIT THOSE THIGHS!
I CAN'T BELIEVE...
ALL THAT LUSCIOUS BABY FLESH IS JUST FROM MY BOOB MILK!

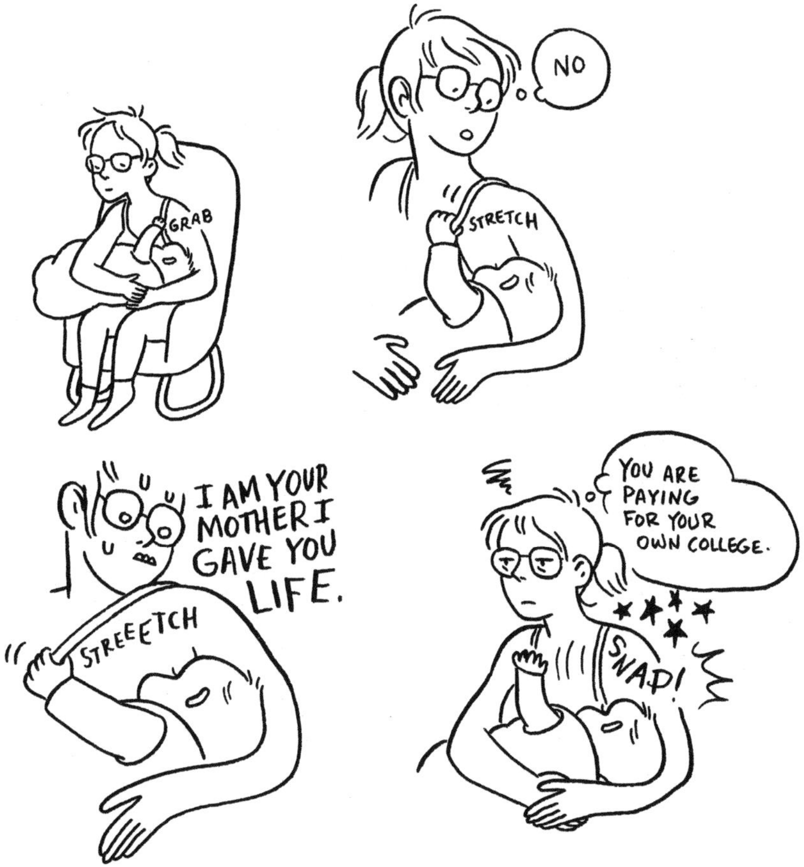
GRAB
NO
STRETCH
I AM YOUR MOTHER I GAVE YOU LIFE.
STREEETCH
YOU ARE PAYING FOR YOUR OWN COLLEGE.
SNAP!

HAHAHA THAT'S RIGHT, SWEETIE! JUST LIKE MAMA'S!
MAMA!
MINE ARE USEFUL!

HEAVY
WITH
CUTENESS
* & ALSO WEIGHT

OH, DID YOU WANT SOME OF MY SANDWICH?

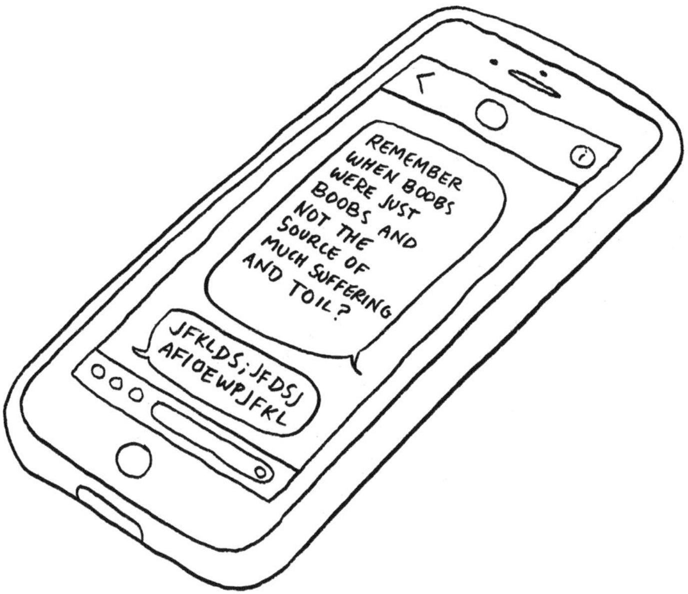
REMEMBER WHEN BOOBS WERE JUST BOOBS AND NOT THE SOURCE OF MUCH SUFFERING AND TOIL?
JFKLDS;JFDSJ AFIOEWPJFKL

PARENTS
ARE PEOPLE

PARENTING
ADVICE

PARENTING
ADVICE
THAT SAYS
THE EXACT
OPPOSITE

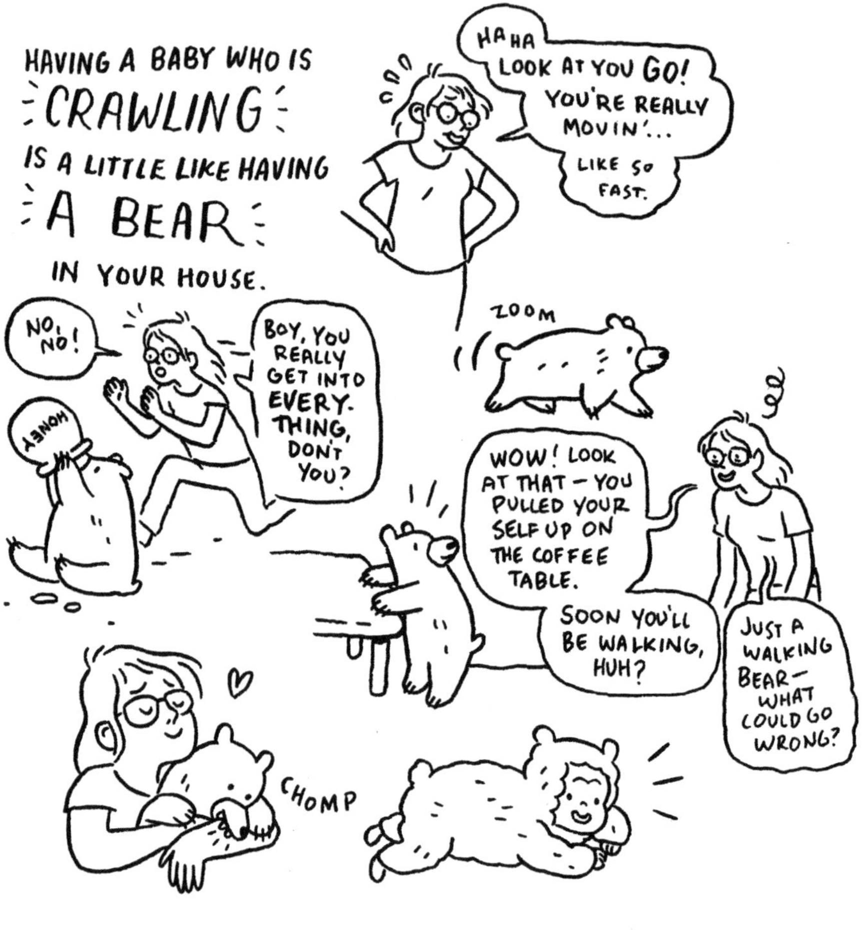
HAVING A BABY WHO IS CRAWLING IS A LITTLE LIKE HAVING A BEAR IN YOUR HOUSE.
HA HA LOOK AT YOU GO! YOU'RE REALLY MOVIN'...
LIKE SO FAST.
ZOOM
NO, NO!
HONEY
BOY, YOU REALLY GET INTO EVERY-THING, DON'T YOU?
WOW! LOOK AT THAT — YOU PULLED YOURSELF UP ON THE COFFEE TABLE.
SOON YOU'LL BE WALKING, HUH?
JUST A WALKING BEAR— WHAT COULD GO WRONG?
CHOMP

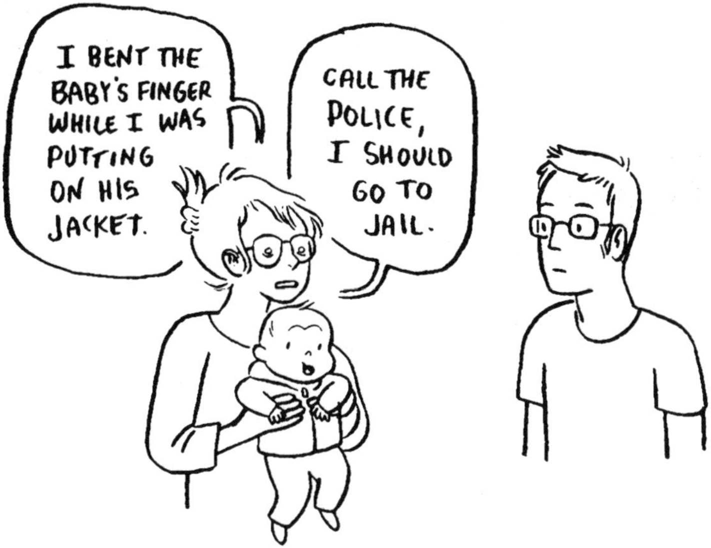
I BENT THE BABY'S FINGER WHILE I WAS PUTTING ON HIS JACKET.
CALL THE POLICE, I SHOULD GO TO JAIL.

MY MOM IS VERY
EXCITED TO SHOW
OFF HER GRANDSON
TO ALL HER FRIENDS.

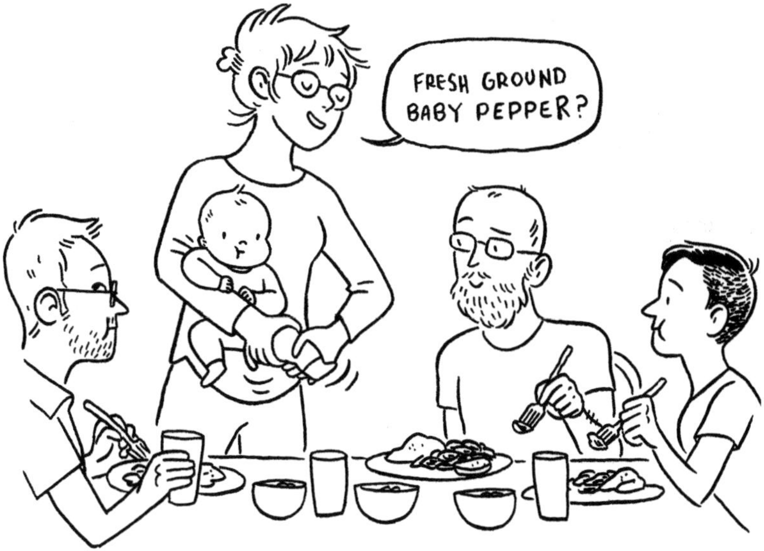
FRESH GROUND BABY PEPPER?

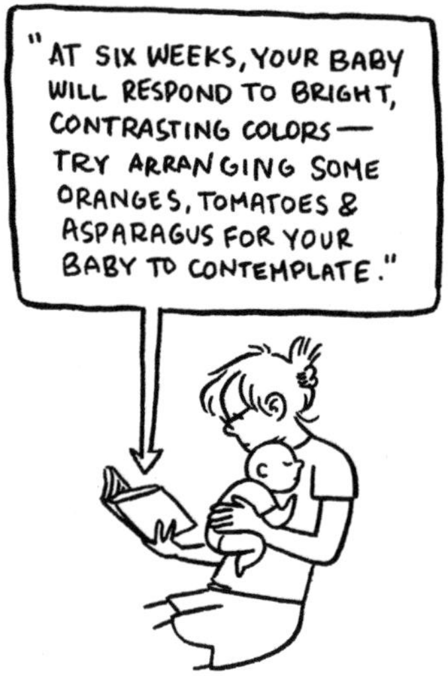
"AT SIX WEEKS, YOUR BABY WILL RESPOND TO BRIGHT, CONTRASTING COLORS— TRY ARRANGING SOME ORANGES, TOMATOES & ASPARAGUS FOR YOUR BABY TO CONTEMPLATE."

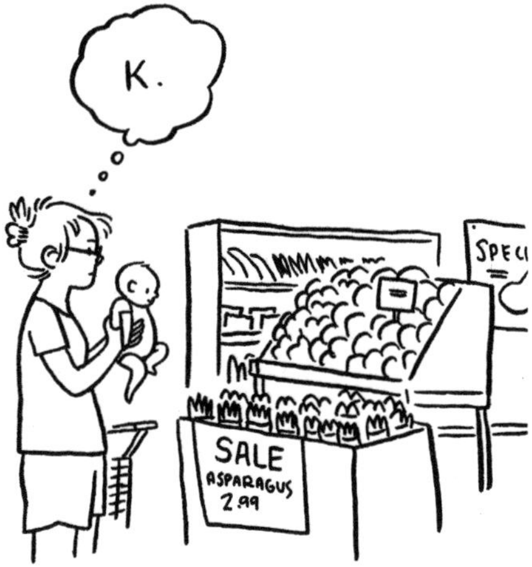
K.
SPEC
SALE
ASPARAGUS
2.99

WHEN YOU HAVE
A BABY, YOU ARE
CONSTANTLY PROCESSING
THE CUTEST THING
YOU'VE EVER SEEN.

OMG.

LA
LA
LA

JUST WHEN YOU THINK:
OK—THERE'S NO WAY
ANYTHING CAN TOP
THAT CUTENESS.

AAAA!

GA?

YOU'RE FACED WITH
SOMETHING THAT'S
LIKE TEN TIMES
CUTER!

HOW?!

ZZZ

IT KINDA READJUSTS YOUR
CUTENESS BAROMETER...

SO
WHAT?

KITTEN & PUPPY
ARE BEST FRIENDS

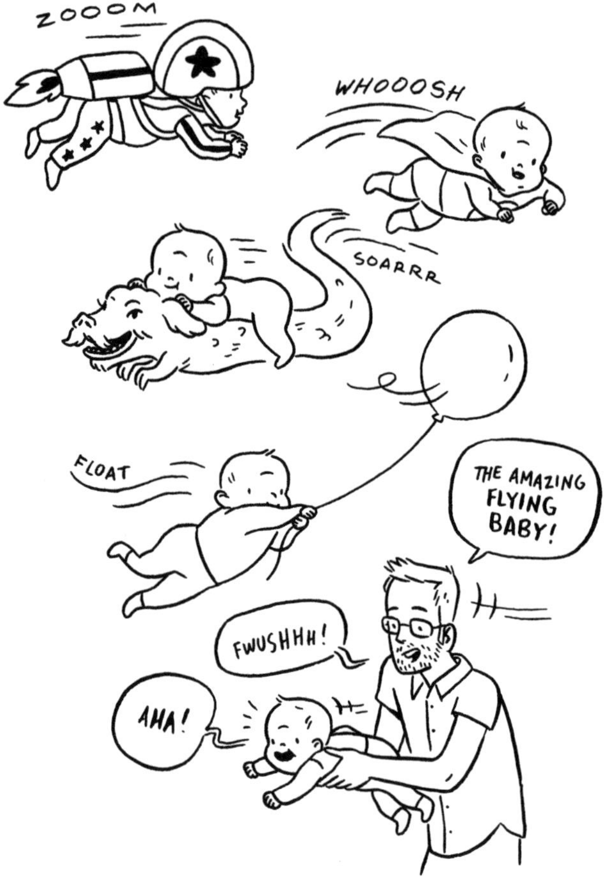
ZOOOM
WHOOOSH
SOARRR
FLOAT
THE AMAZING FLYING BABY!
FWUSHHH!
AHA!

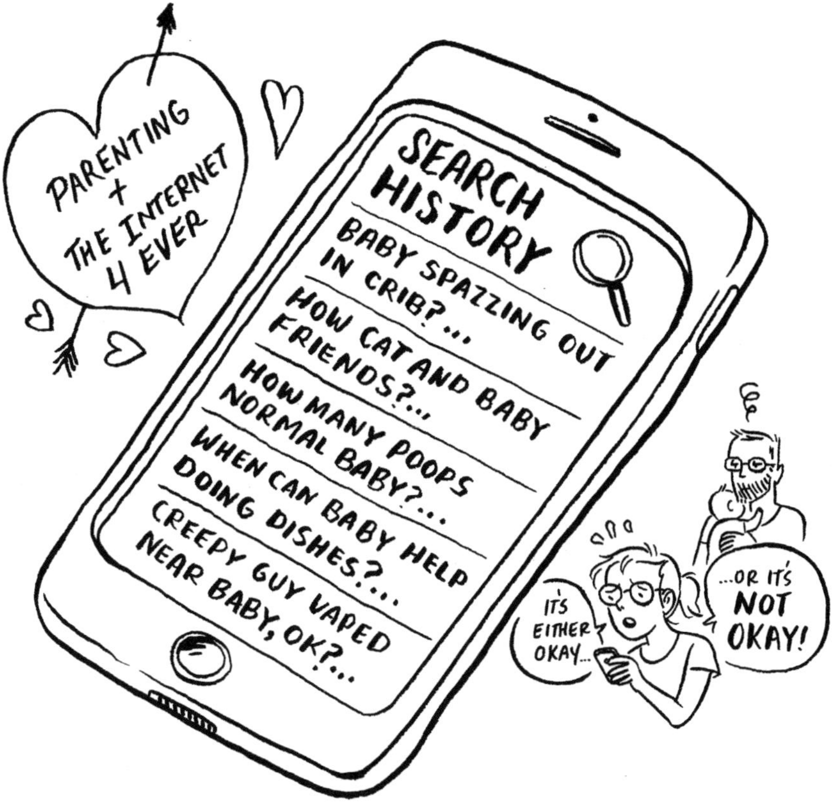
PARENTING + THE INTERNET 4 EVER
SEARCH HISTORY
BABY SPAZZING OUT IN CRIB?...
HOW CAT AND BABY FRIENDS?...
HOW MANY POOPS NORMAL BABY?...
WHEN CAN BABY HELP DOING DISHES?...
CREEPY GUY VAPED NEAR BABY, OK?...
IT'S EITHER OKAY...
...OR IT'S NOT OKAY!

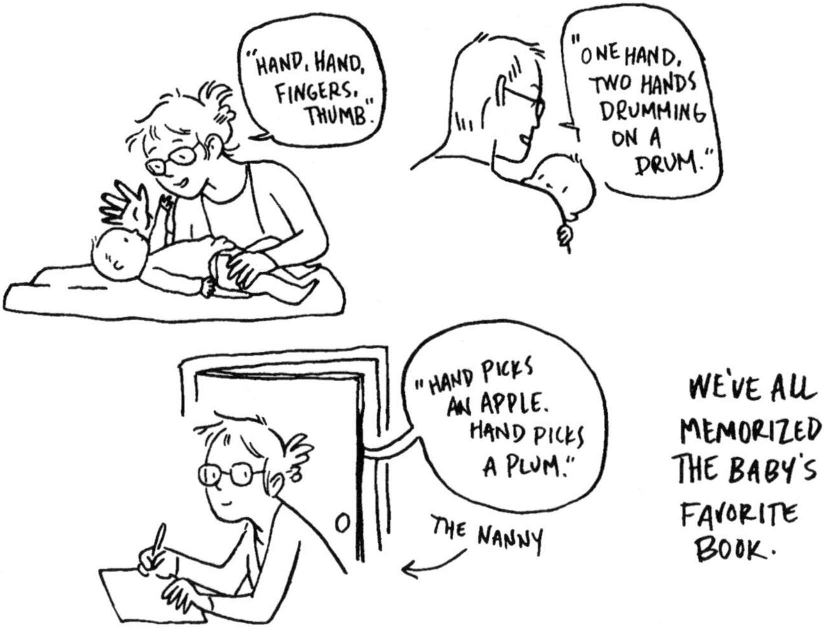
"HAND, HAND, FINGERS, THUMB."
"ONE HAND, TWO HANDS DRUMMING ON A DRUM."
"HAND PICKS AN APPLE. HAND PICKS A PLUM."
THE NANNY
WE'VE ALL MEMORIZED THE BABY'S FAVORITE BOOK.

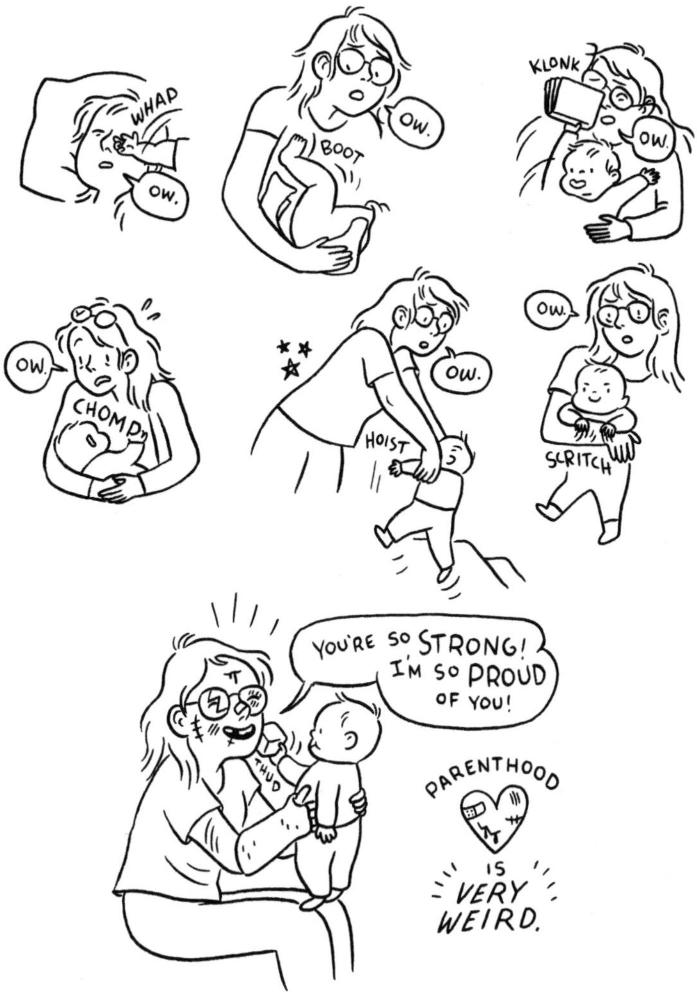
WHAP
OW.
BOOT
OW.
KLONK
OW.
OW.
CHOMP
OW.
HOIST
OW.
SCRITCH
YOU'RE SO STRONG! I'M SO PROUD OF YOU!
THUD
PARENTHOOD IS VERY WEIRD.

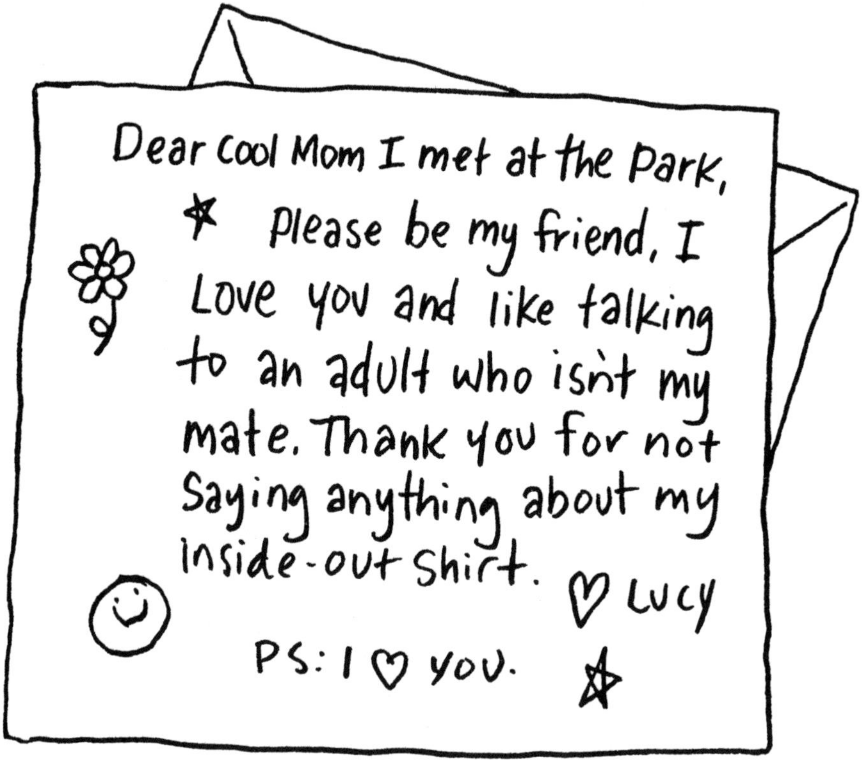
Dear cool Mom I met at the Park,
Please be my friend, I Love you and like talking to an adult who isn't my mate. Thank you for not Saying anything about my inside-out Shirt.
♡ Lucy
PS: I ♡ you.

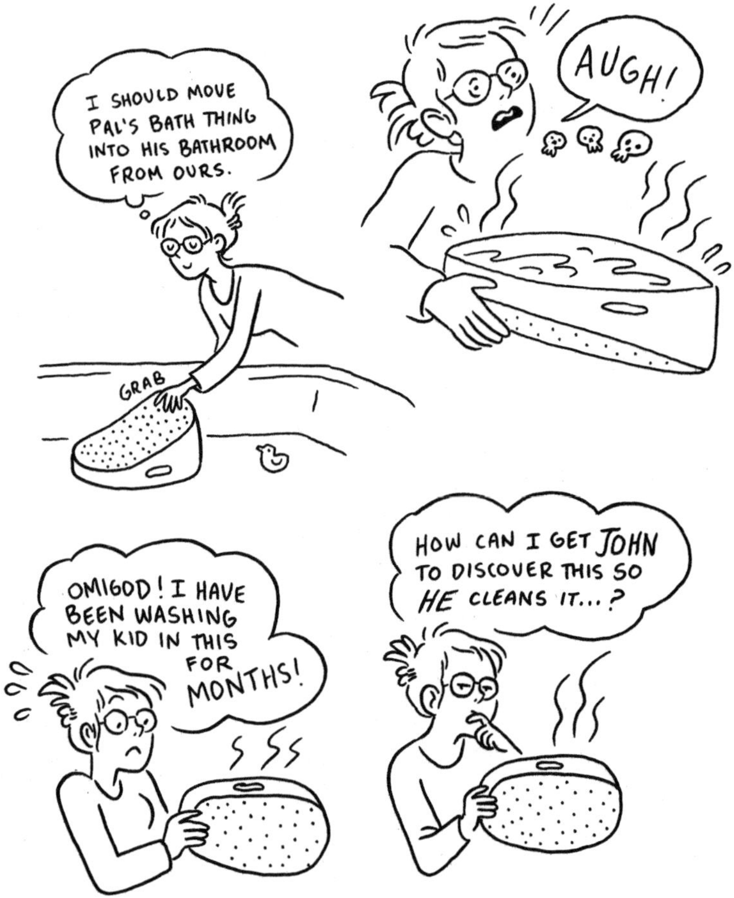
I SHOULD MOVE PAL'S BATH THING INTO HIS BATHROOM FROM OURS.
GRAB
AUGH!
OMIGOD! I HAVE BEEN WASHING MY KID IN THIS FOR MONTHS!
HOW CAN I GET JOHN TO DISCOVER THIS SO HE CLEANS IT...?

SOME UNEXPECTED ASPECTS OF

·MOMMIFICATION·

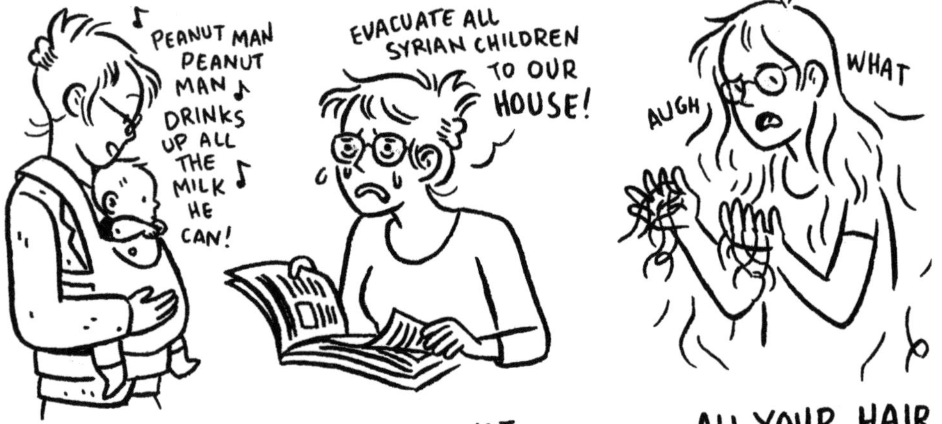

PEANUT MAN PEANUT MAN DRINKS UP ALL THE MILK HE CAN!
EVACUATE ALL SYRIAN CHILDREN TO OUR HOUSE!
AUGH
WHAT

YOU ARE TOTALLY UNSELFCONSCIOUS ABOUT MAKING UP SONGS & SINGING THEM IN PUBLIC.

YOU CANNOT HEAR ABOUT ANYTHING BAD HAPPENING TO A KID WITH-OUT GETTING MESSED UP FOR DAYS.

ALL YOUR HAIR FALLS OUT LIKE YOU'RE A GIANT DOG IN SPRINGTIME.

PEOPLE SURE DO
HAVE A LOTTA OPINIONS
ABOUT PARENTING.

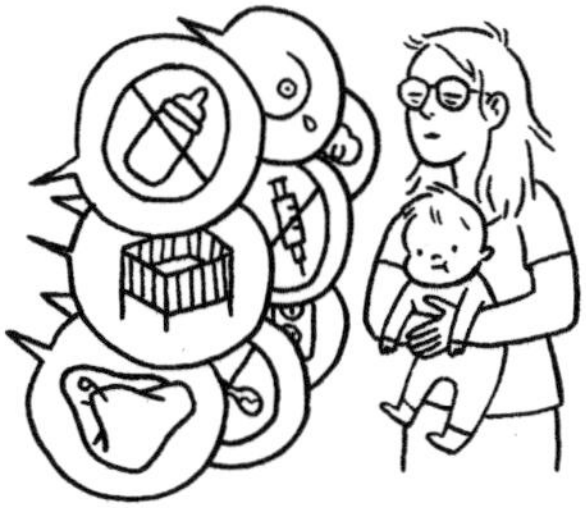

THE IRONY IS
THAT AFTER YEARS
OF WORRYING ABOUT
WHAT OTHER PEOPLE THINK...

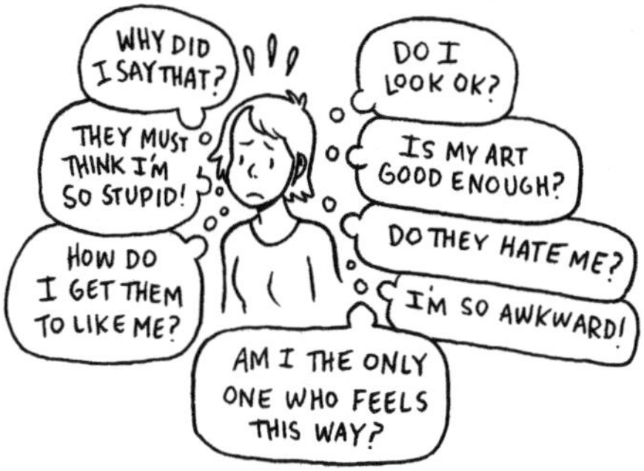
WHY DID I SAY THAT?
DO I LOOK OK?
THEY MUST THINK I'M SO STUPID!
IS MY ART GOOD ENOUGH?
DO THEY HATE ME?
HOW DO I GET THEM TO LIKE ME?
I'M SO AWKWARD!
AM I THE ONLY ONE WHO FEELS THIS WAY?

...THERE'S REALLY ONLY
ONE PERSON'S OPINION
I CARE ABOUT NOW.

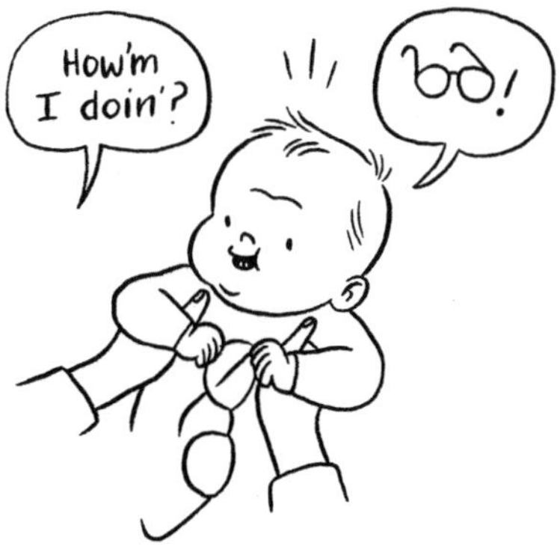
How'm I doin'?

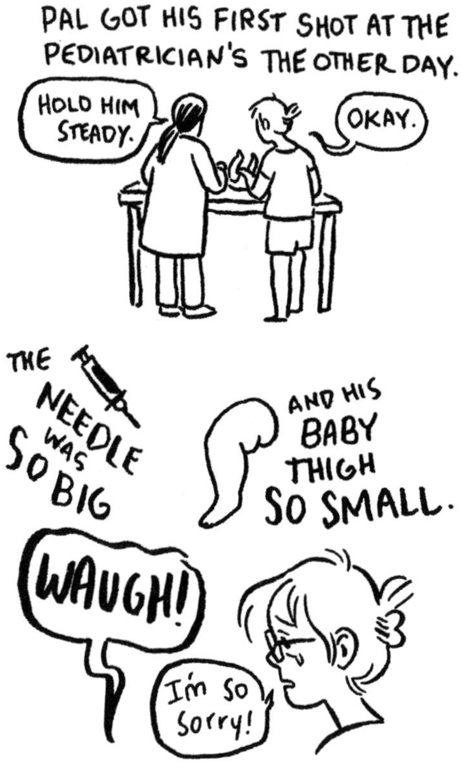
PAL GOT HIS FIRST SHOT AT THE PEDIATRICIAN'S THE OTHER DAY.
HOLD HIM STEADY.
OKAY.
THE NEEDLE WAS SO BIG
AND HIS BABY THIGH SO SMALL.
WAUGH!
I'm so sorry!

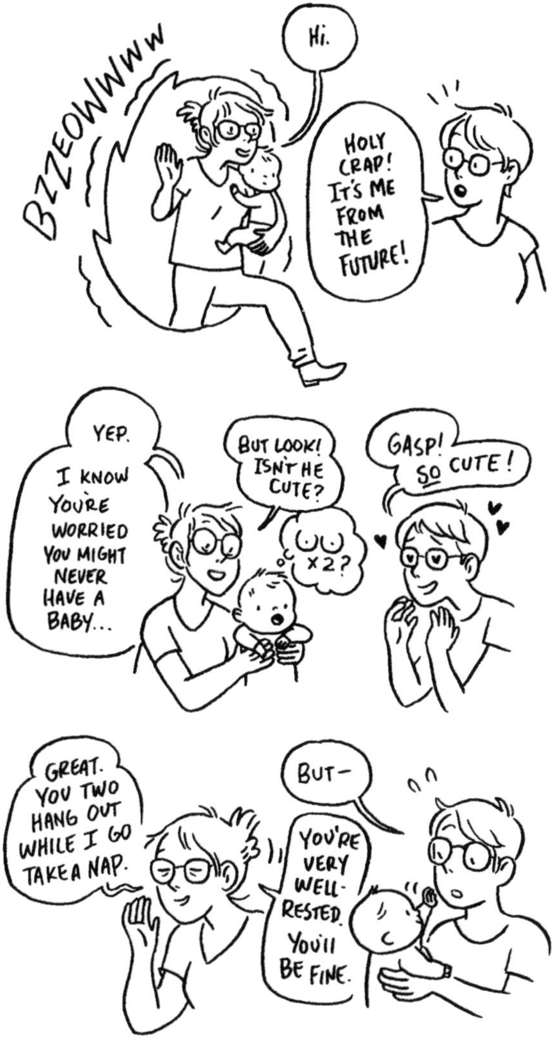
BZZEOWWWW
Hi.
HOLY CRAP! IT'S ME FROM THE FUTURE!
YEP.
I KNOW YOU'RE WORRIED YOU MIGHT NEVER HAVE A BABY...
BUT LOOK! ISN'T HE CUTE?
GASP! SO CUTE!
×2?
GREAT. YOU TWO HANG OUT WHILE I GO TAKE A NAP.
BUT-
YOU'RE VERY WELL-RESTED. YOU'LL BE FINE.

$150

$FREE

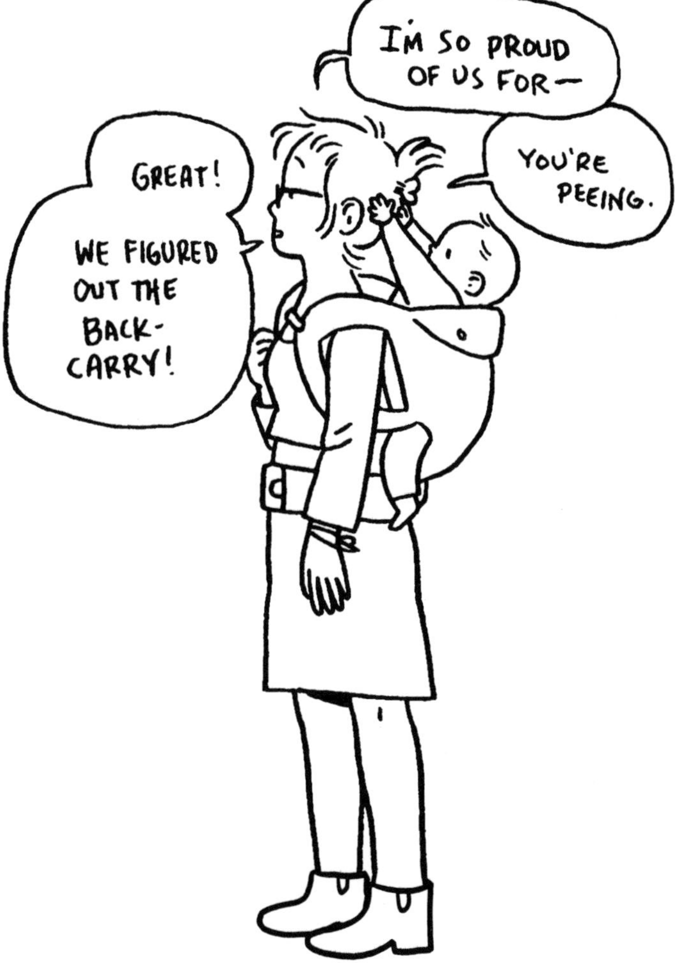
GREAT!
WE FIGURED OUT THE BACK-CARRY!
I'M SO PROUD OF US FOR—
YOU'RE PEEING.

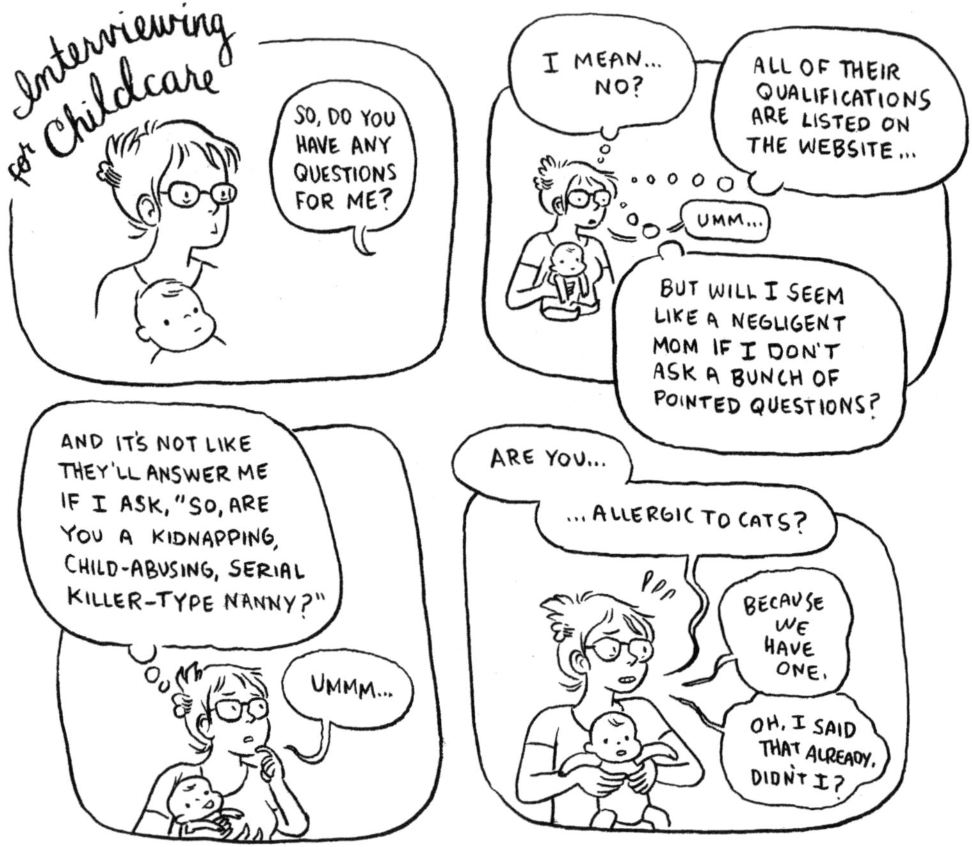
Interviewing for Childcare
SO, DO YOU HAVE ANY QUESTIONS FOR ME?
I MEAN... NO?
ALL OF THEIR QUALIFICATIONS ARE LISTED ON THE WEBSITE...
UMM...
BUT WILL I SEEM LIKE A NEGLIGENT MOM IF I DON'T ASK A BUNCH OF POINTED QUESTIONS?
AND IT'S NOT LIKE THEY'LL ANSWER ME IF I ASK, "SO, ARE YOU A KIDNAPPING, CHILD-ABUSING, SERIAL KILLER-TYPE NANNY?"
UMMM...
ARE YOU...
...ALLERGIC TO CATS?
BECAUSE WE HAVE ONE.
OH, I SAID THAT ALREADY, DIDN'T I?

I LIKE TO
MAKE THE
BABY
PEER OUT
FROM
IMPROBABLE
PLACES
AROUND
THE HOUSE.

PARENTAL NEOLOGISM

"MELOPROPISM"

MISTAKENLY FINDING YOURSELF SINGING A WILDLY INAPPROPRIATE SONG TO YOUR YOUNG CHILD.

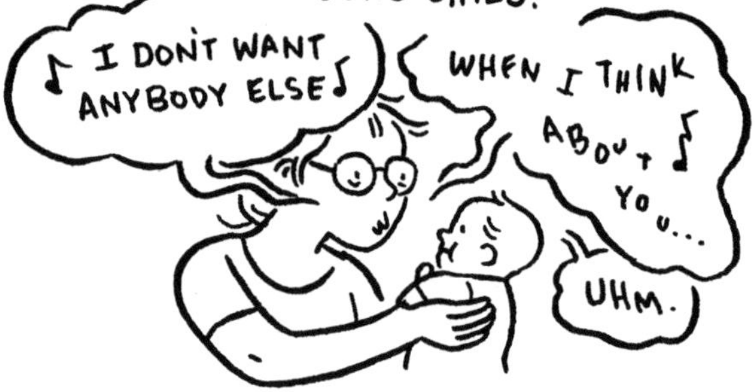
I DON'T WANT ANYBODY ELSE
WHEN I THINK ABOUT YOU...
UHM.

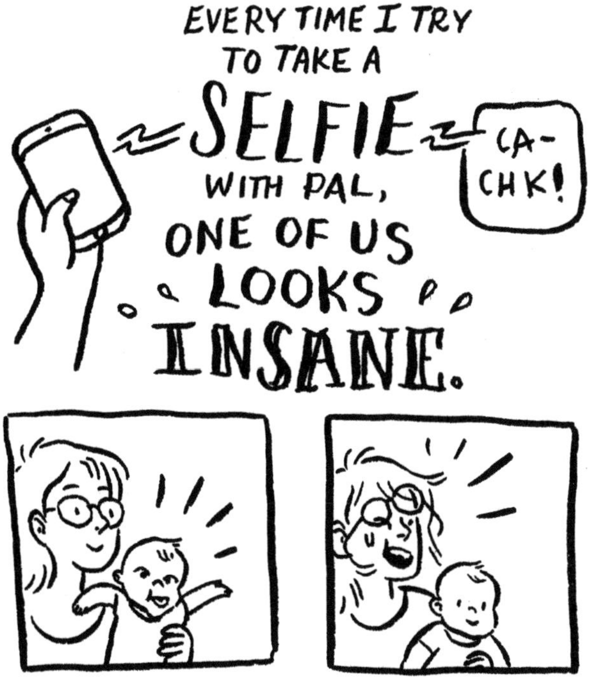
EVERY TIME I TRY TO TAKE A SELFIE WITH PAL, ONE OF US LOOKS INSANE.
CA-CHK!

There are lots of maternity gift guides...

NO, BUT

For Real,

THESE ARE MY

New Mom Necessities:

FLOWERS Are Also Quite Nice.

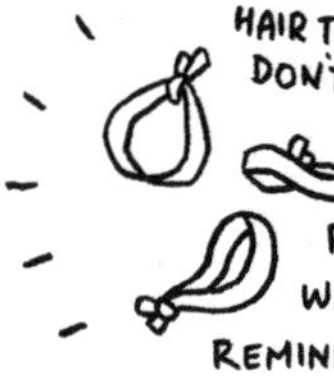

THOSE RIBBONY HAIR TIES THAT DON'T WORK ON PONYTAILS BUT LOOK PRETTY ON WRISTS TO REMIND YOU WHICH BOOB YOU NURSED ON LAST.

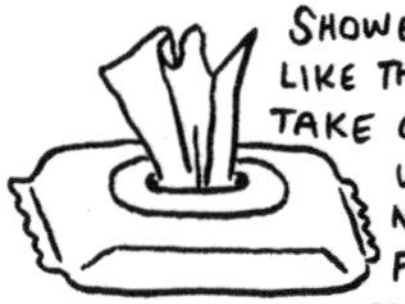

SHOWER CLOTHS, LIKE THE KIND YOU TAKE CAMPING, FOR WHEN YOU GET NIGHT SWEATS FROM BREAST-FEEDING HORMONES. MAKE YOU SMELLY, BUT YOU CAN STILL GET A SHOWERLESS DAY OUT OF YOUR HAIR.

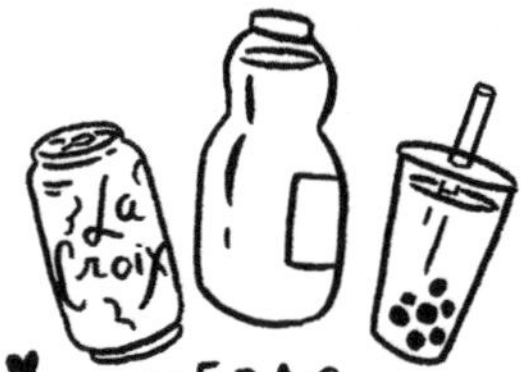
La Croix

♥ BEVERAGES ♥

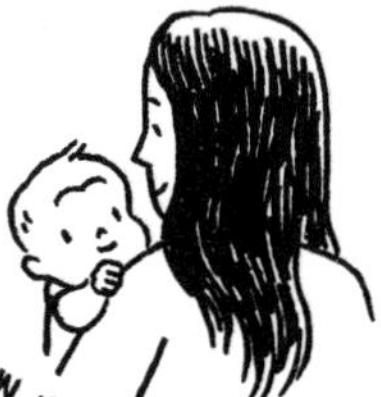

♡ A FEW HOURS OF NANNY TIME. ♡

HARVEST
•DAY•
AT THE
GARFIELD
PARK
CONSERVATORY

A CALABASH FRUIT IS EXACTLY THE SIZE OF THE BABY'S HEAD.

WATCHING THE FISH

DON'T DROP

COOL FISH

ZZZ

NOT INTERESTED IN PETTING THE CHICKEN

THIS LEAF IS SO BIG, THE BABY COULD USE IT AS A BOAT.

PUT THOSE CITY BABY FEET IN THE GRASS!

NICE SMELLS EVERYWHERE

CACTI WITH GRANDMA

ALSO DON'T DROP

SNRK
?
MFF
?
SHR UG

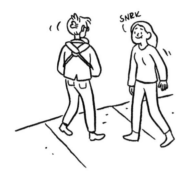

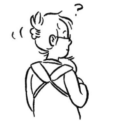

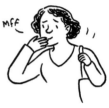

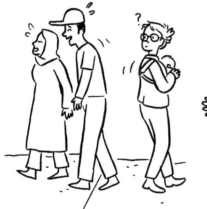

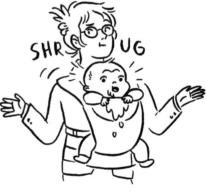

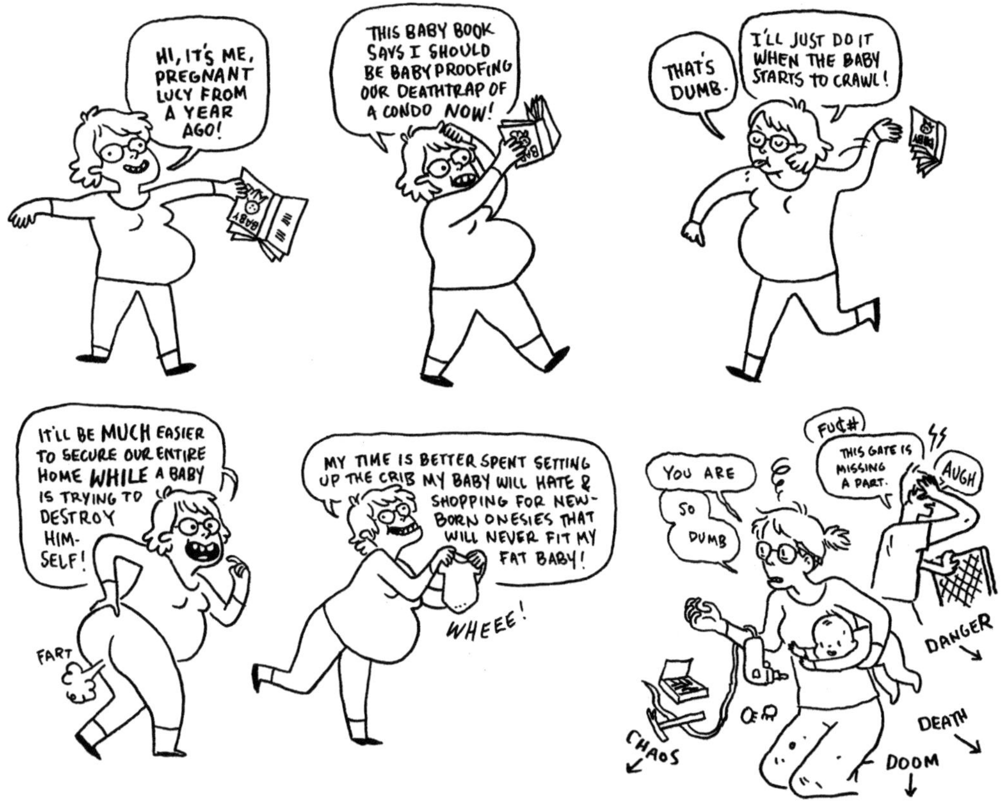
HI, IT'S ME, PREGNANT LUCY FROM A YEAR AGO!
BABY
THIS BABY BOOK SAYS I SHOULD BE BABY PROOFING OUR DEATHTRAP OF A CONDO NOW!
THAT'S DUMB.
I'LL JUST DO IT WHEN THE BABY STARTS TO CRAWL!
IT'LL BE MUCH EASIER TO SECURE OUR ENTIRE HOME WHILE A BABY IS TRYING TO DESTROY HIM-SELF!
FART
MY TIME IS BETTER SPENT SETTING UP THE CRIB MY BABY WILL HATE & SHOPPING FOR NEW-BORN ONESIES THAT WILL NEVER FIT MY FAT BABY!
WHEEE!
FU¢#
THIS GATE IS MISSING A PART.
AUGH
YOU ARE
SO
DUMB
DANGER
DEATH
DOOM
CHAOS

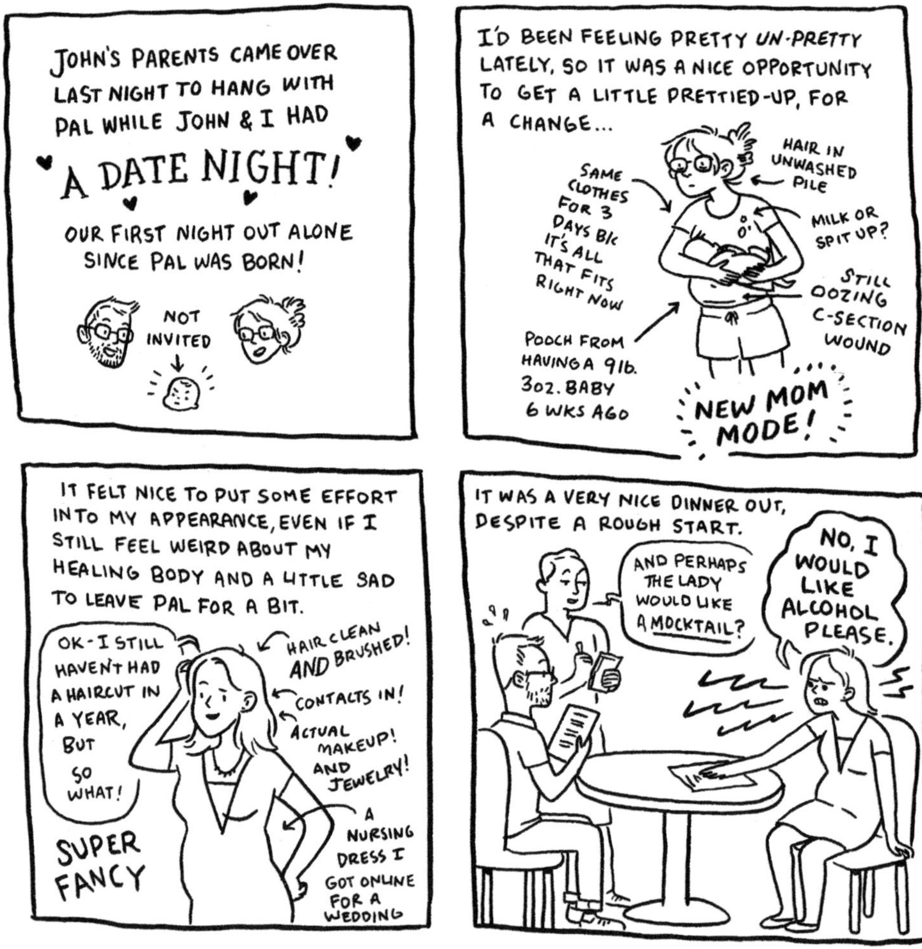
JOHN'S PARENTS CAME OVER LAST NIGHT TO HANG WITH PAL WHILE JOHN & I HAD
A DATE NIGHT!
OUR FIRST NIGHT OUT ALONE SINCE PAL WAS BORN!
NOT INVITED
I'D BEEN FEELING PRETTY UN-PRETTY LATELY, SO IT WAS A NICE OPPORTUNITY TO GET A LITTLE PRETTIED-UP, FOR A CHANGE...
SAME CLOTHES FOR 3 DAYS B/C IT'S ALL THAT FITS RIGHT NOW
HAIR IN UNWASHED PILE
MILK OR SPIT UP?
STILL OOZING C-SECTION WOUND
POOCH FROM HAVING A 9lb. 3oz. BABY 6 WKS AGO
NEW MOM MODE!
IT FELT NICE TO PUT SOME EFFORT INTO MY APPEARANCE, EVEN IF I STILL FEEL WEIRD ABOUT MY HEALING BODY AND A LITTLE SAD TO LEAVE PAL FOR A BIT.
OK - I STILL HAVEN'T HAD A HAIRCUT IN A YEAR, BUT SO WHAT!
HAIR CLEAN AND BRUSHED!
CONTACTS IN!
ACTUAL MAKEUP! AND JEWELRY!
A NURSING DRESS I GOT ONLINE FOR A WEDDING
SUPER FANCY
IT WAS A VERY NICE DINNER OUT, DESPITE A ROUGH START.
AND PERHAPS THE LADY WOULD LIKE A MOCKTAIL?
NO, I WOULD LIKE ALCOHOL PLEASE.

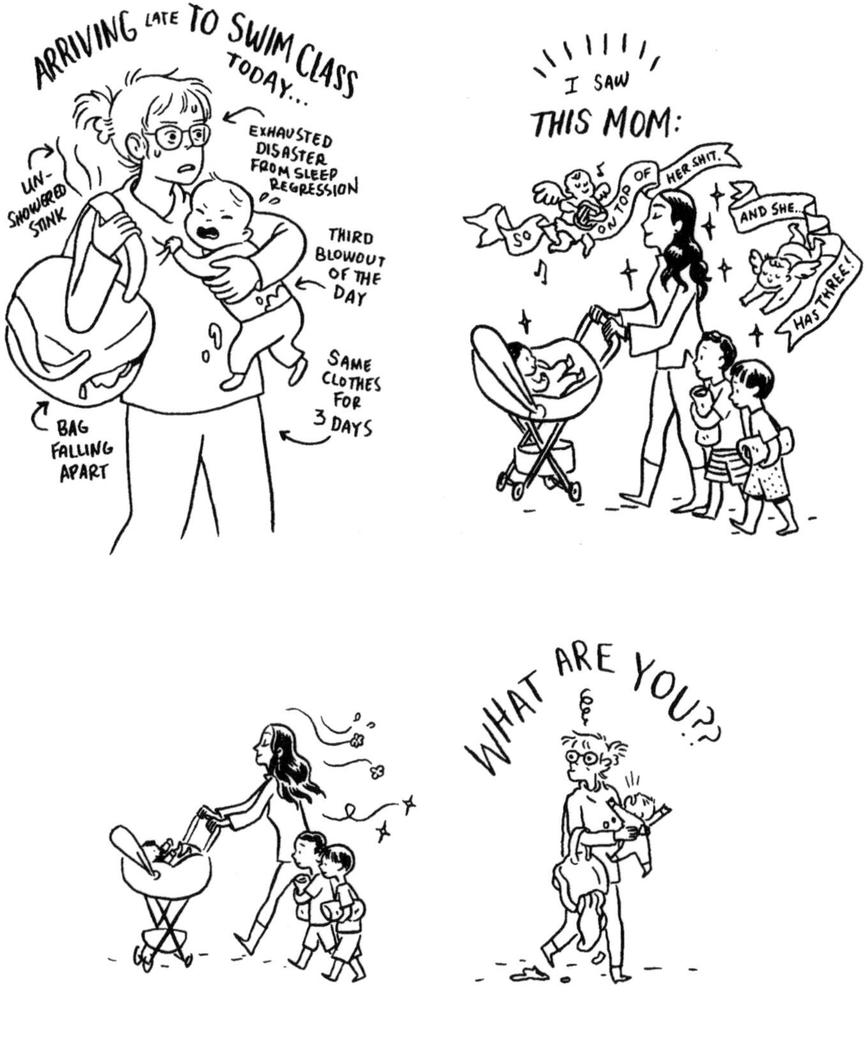
ARRIVING LATE TO SWIM CLASS TODAY...
UN-SHOWERED STINK
EXHAUSTED DISASTER FROM SLEEP REGRESSION
THIRD BLOWOUT OF THE DAY
SAME CLOTHES FOR 3 DAYS
BAG FALLING APART
I SAW
THIS MOM:
SO ON TOP OF HER SHIT.
AND SHE...
HAS THREE!
WHAT ARE YOU??

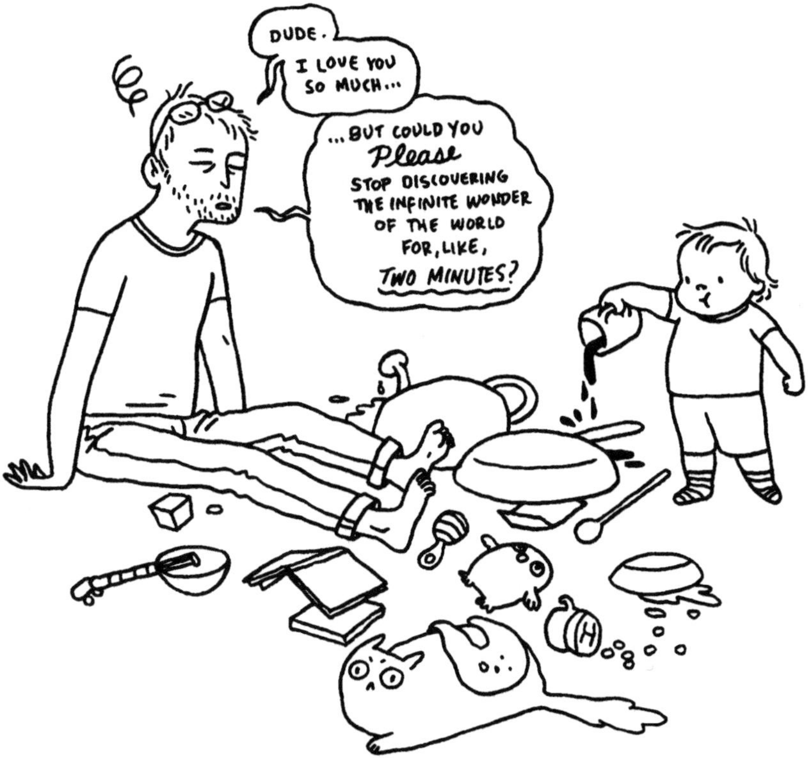
DUDE.
I LOVE YOU SO MUCH...
...BUT COULD YOU *Please* STOP DISCOVERING THE INFINITE WONDER OF THE WORLD FOR, LIKE, TWO MINUTES?

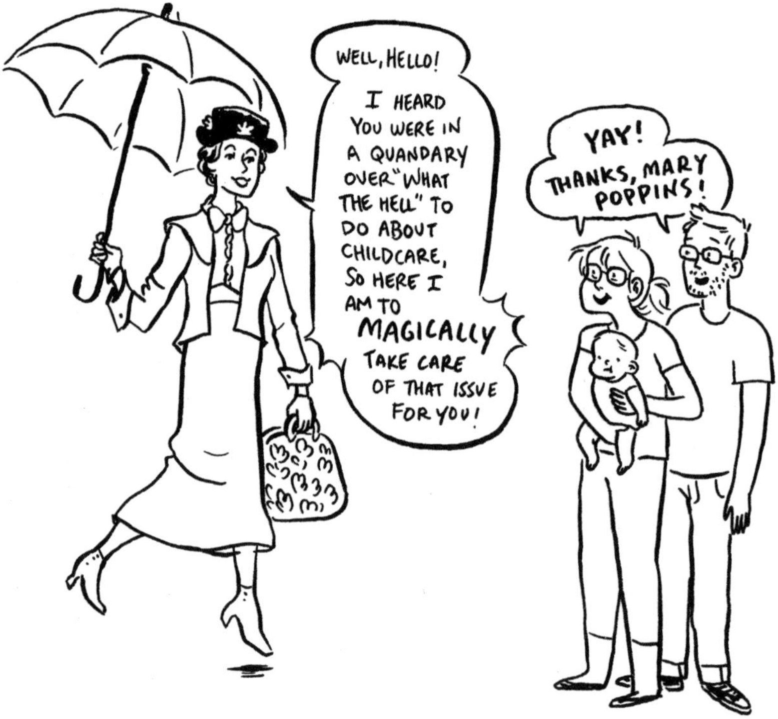
WELL, HELLO!
I HEARD YOU WERE IN A QUANDARY OVER "WHAT THE HELL" TO DO ABOUT CHILDCARE, SO HERE I AM TO MAGICALLY TAKE CARE OF THAT ISSUE FOR YOU!
YAY! THANKS, MARY POPPINS!

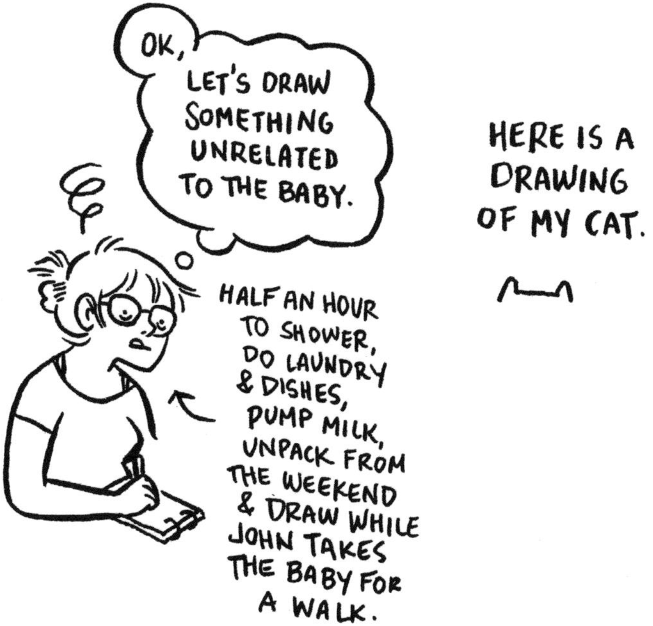
OK, LET'S DRAW SOMETHING UNRELATED TO THE BABY.
HALF AN HOUR TO SHOWER, DO LAUNDRY & DISHES, PUMP MILK, UNPACK FROM THE WEEKEND & DRAW WHILE JOHN TAKES THE BABY FOR A WALK.
HERE IS A DRAWING OF MY CAT.

BODILY FLUIDS

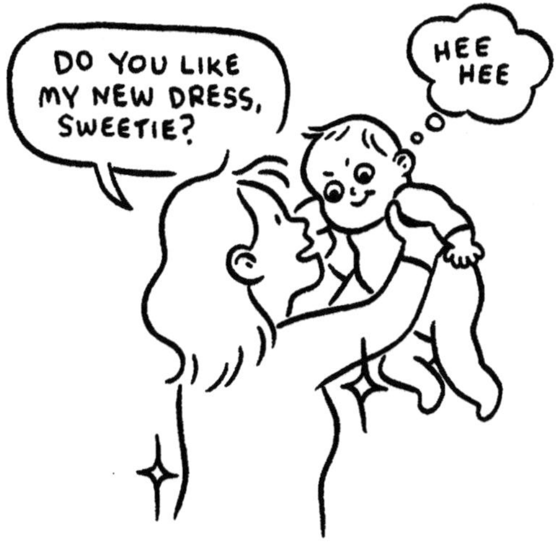
DO YOU LIKE MY NEW DRESS, SWEETIE?
HEE HEE

Nov 30, 2016

Dear Son,

Today you pooped through four outfits. Please teach me about future technology with the same patience I showed you when putting you in your fifth clean onesie. Love,
Mama

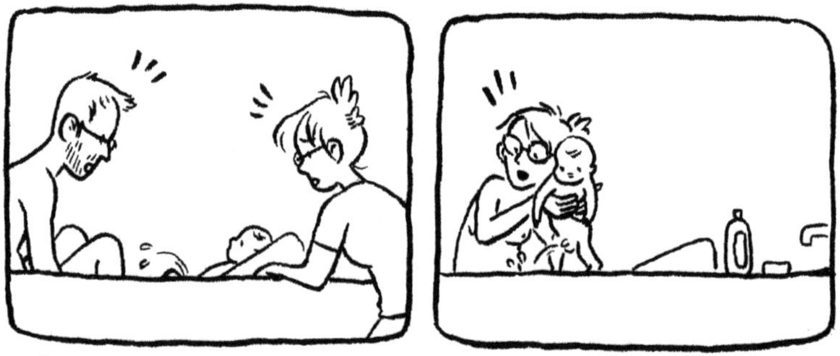

SO FAR, PAL HAS PEED IN EVERY BATH HE'S HAD.

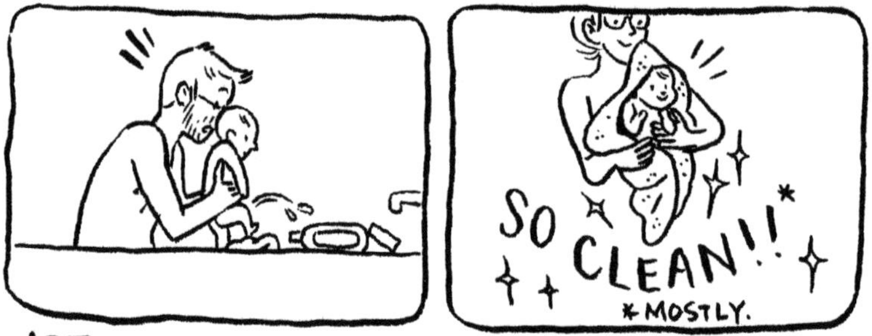
SO CLEAN!!*
*MOSTLY.

AT THIS POINT, WE CALL IT A WIN WHEN THERE'S NO POOP.

NOW THAT MY COLD
IS GETTING BETTER,

SNIFF
SSNIFFF

I'M FINALLY REGAINING
MY SENSE OF SMELL.

IT HAD BEEN GONE
FOR OVER A
WEEK

& I
MISSED
THE
SMELL
OF THE
BABY'S
HEAD.

...BUT ALSO...

I'M GLAD
IT'S COMING
BACK...

YOGURT
FROM
BREAKFAST

HERE BE
MONSTERS

SHIRT STILL
SMELLS LIKE
BARF AFTER
TWO WASHES!

HOW CAN YOU
STED IN SOMETHING
WHEN YOU CAN'T
WALK YET?

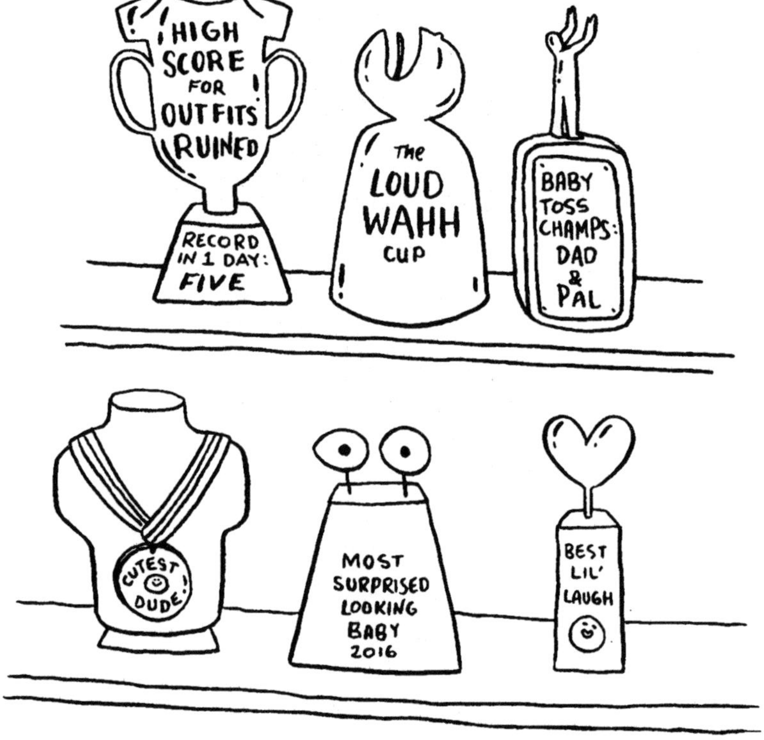
HIGH SCORE FOR OUTFITS RUINED
RECORD IN 1 DAY: FIVE
THE LOUD WAHH CUP
BABY TOSS CHAMPS: DAD & PAL
CUTEST DUDE
MOST SURPRISED LOOKING BABY 2016
BEST LIL' LAUGH

HOW MANY
TIMES CAN
ONE BABY
BLOW OUT
IN THE FLOOR SEAT?

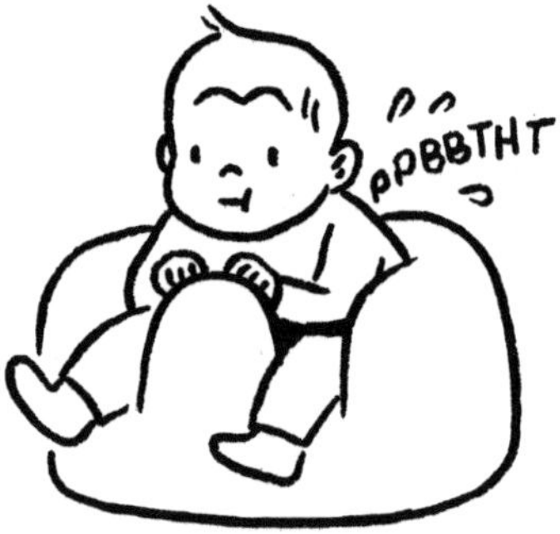
PPBBTHT

ANSWER:
FIVE
SO FAR!

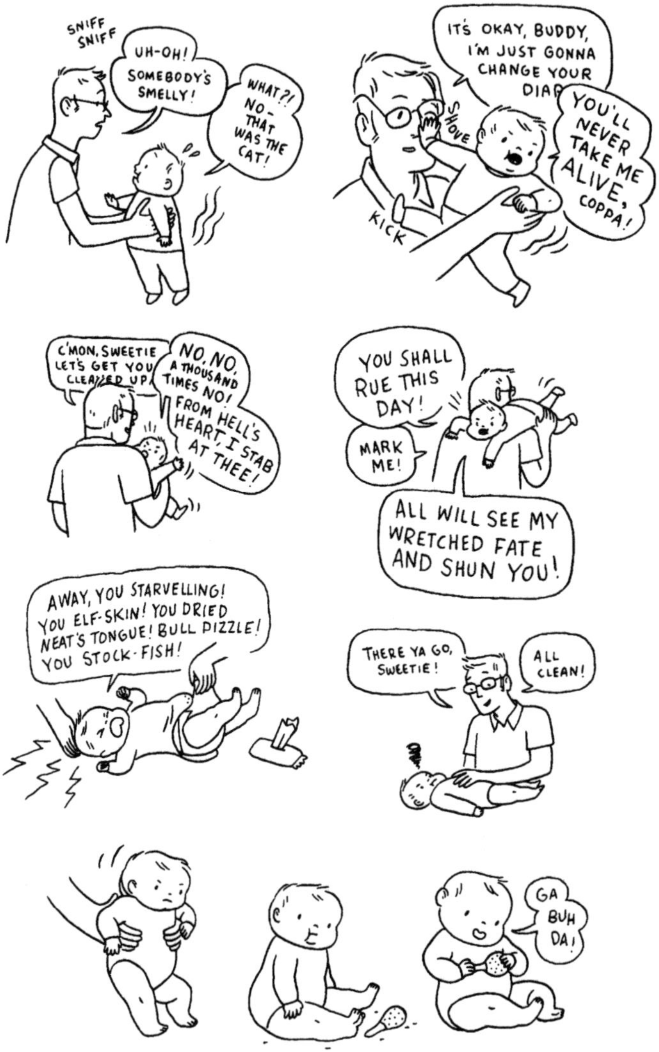
SNIFF SNIFF
UH-OH! SOMEBODY'S SMELLY!
WHAT?! NO – THAT WAS THE CAT!
IT'S OKAY, BUDDY, I'M JUST GONNA CHANGE YOUR DIAP
SHOVE
YOU'LL NEVER TAKE ME ALIVE, COPPA!
KICK
C'MON, SWEETIE LET'S GET YOU
NO, NO, A THOUSAND TIMES NO!
FROM HELL'S HEART, I STAB AT THEE!
YOU SHALL RUE THIS DAY!
MARK ME!
ALL WILL SEE MY WRETCHED FATE AND SHUN YOU!
AWAY, YOU STARVELLING! YOU ELF-SKIN! YOU DRIED NEAT'S TONGUE! BULL PIZZLE! YOU STOCK-FISH!
THERE YA GO, SWEETIE!
ALL CLEAN!
GA BUH DA!

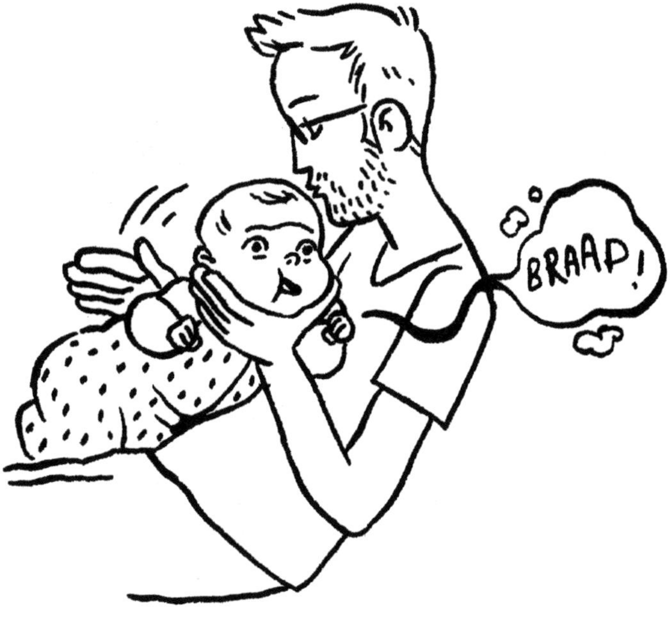
BRAAP!

THE
BABY
HAS A
FEVER.

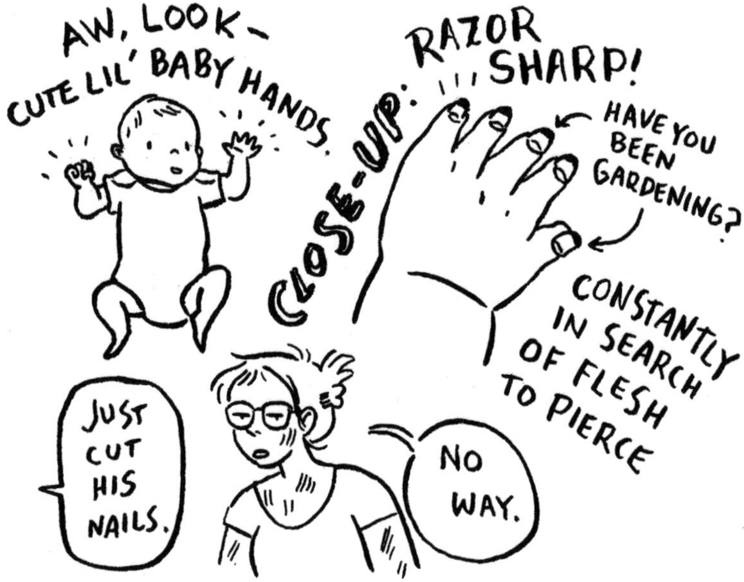

AW, LOOK-
CUTE LIL' BABY HANDS.
CLOSE-UP: RAZOR SHARP!
HAVE YOU BEEN GARDENING?
CONSTANTLY IN SEARCH OF FLESH TO PIERCE
JUST CUT HIS NAILS.
NO WAY.

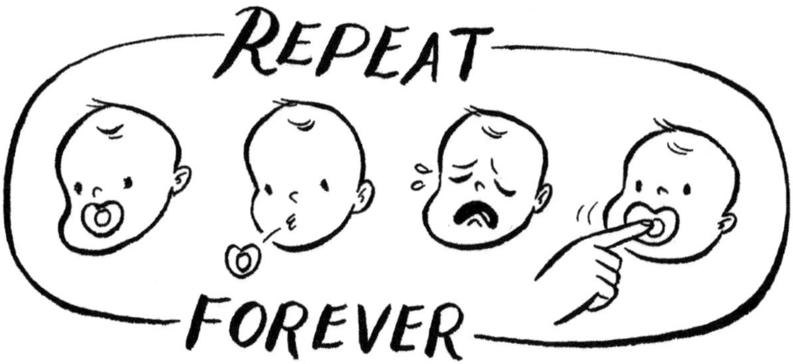
REPEAT
FOREVER

THERE ARE SOME BABY TASKS I LIKE MORE THAN OTHERS...

DIAPERS: SURPRISINGLY DON'T MIND

BATHS: ♥♥♥♥ RAD

NAIL CLIPPING: NOT MY FAVE

BUT THE PEDIATRICIAN RECENTLY TOLD US WE SHOULD BE *BRUSHING HIS TEETH*, AND...

THIS FEELS GENUINELY RIDICULOUS.

YOU HAVE *TWO TEETH*.

WHY IS THIS SO HARD?

THRASH THRASH

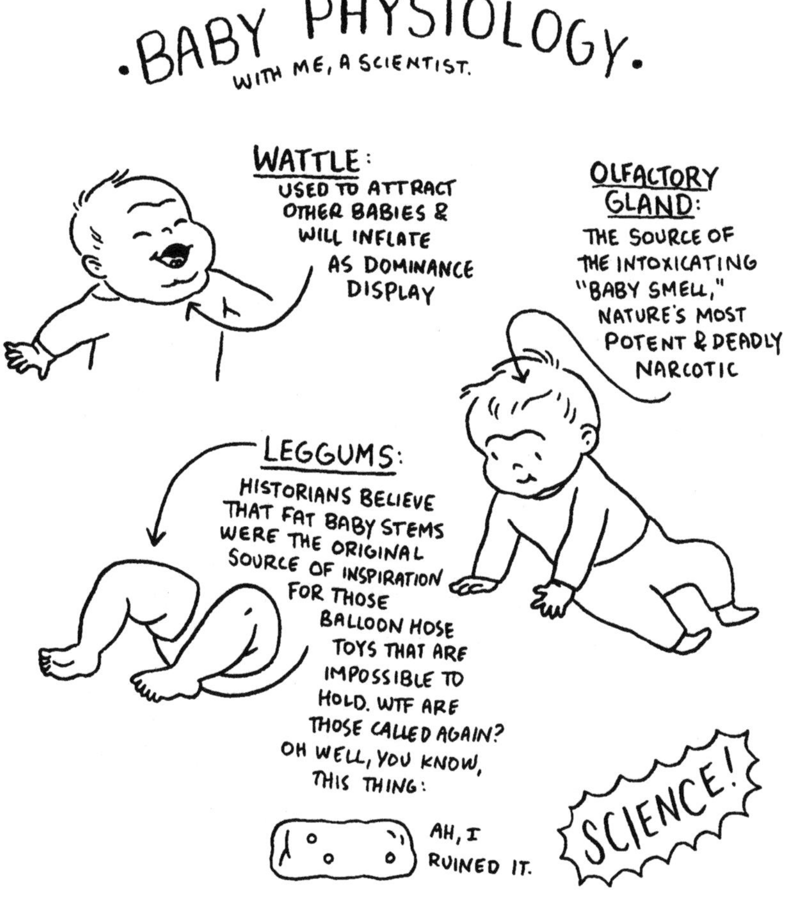

BABY PHYSIOLOGY
WITH ME, A SCIENTIST.
WATTLE: USED TO ATTRACT OTHER BABIES & WILL INFLATE AS DOMINANCE DISPLAY
OLFACTORY GLAND: THE SOURCE OF THE INTOXICATING "BABY SMELL," NATURE'S MOST POTENT & DEADLY NARCOTIC
LEGGUMS: HISTORIANS BELIEVE THAT FAT BABY STEMS WERE THE ORIGINAL SOURCE OF INSPIRATION FOR THOSE BALLOON HOSE TOYS THAT ARE IMPOSSIBLE TO HOLD. WTF ARE THOSE CALLED AGAIN? OH WELL, YOU KNOW, THIS THING:
AH, I RUINED IT.
SCIENCE!

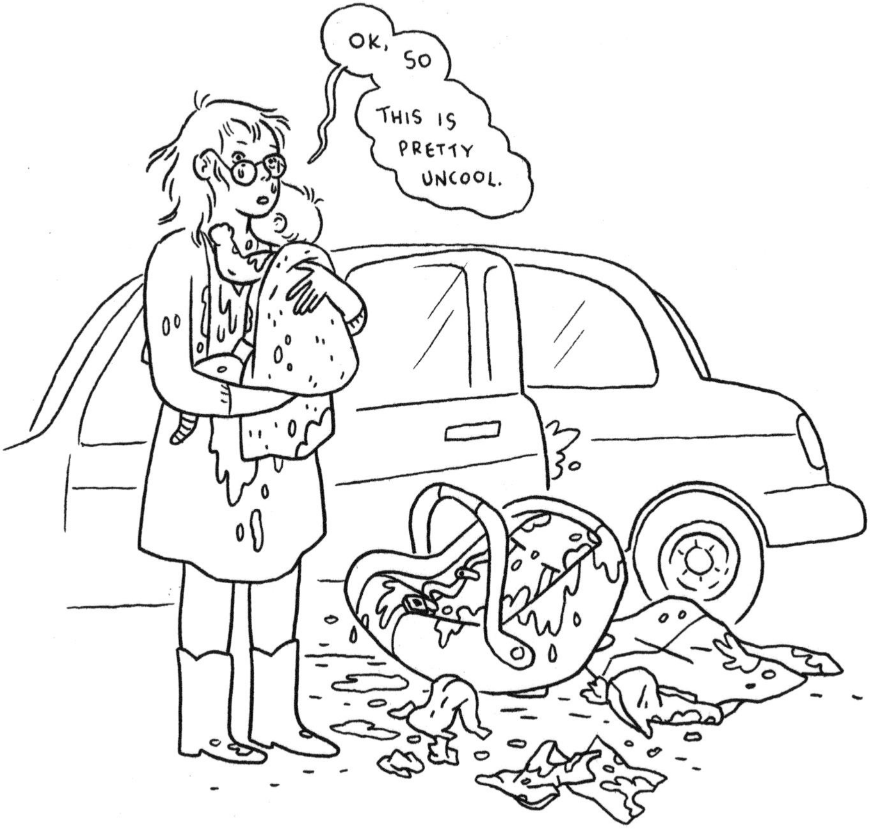
OK, SO
THIS IS PRETTY UNCOOL.

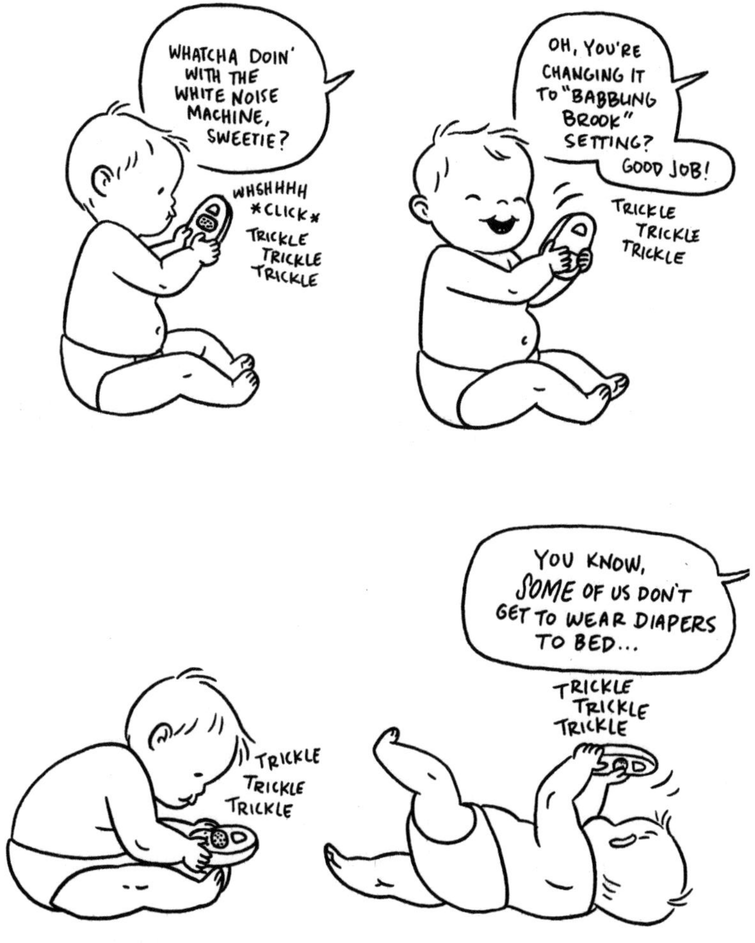
WHATCHA DOIN' WITH THE WHITE NOISE MACHINE, SWEETIE?
WHSHHHH
CLICK
TRICKLE TRICKLE TRICKLE
OH, YOU'RE CHANGING IT TO "BABBLING BROOK" SETTING?
GOOD JOB!
TRICKLE TRICKLE TRICKLE
TRICKLE TRICKLE TRICKLE
YOU KNOW, SOME OF US DON'T GET TO WEAR DIAPERS TO BED...
TRICKLE TRICKLE TRICKLE

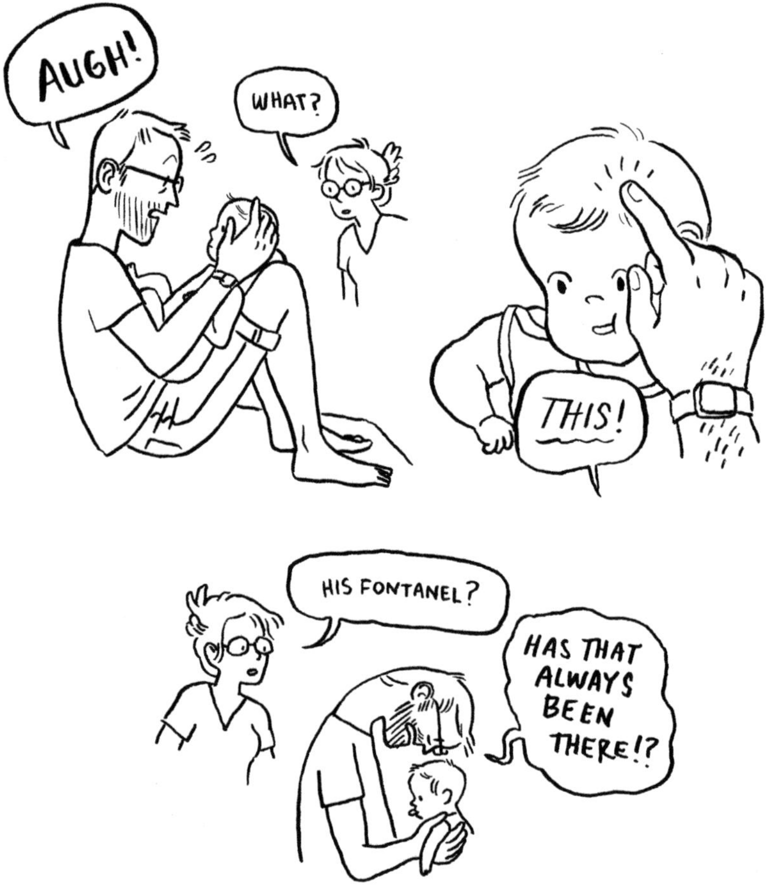
AUGH!
WHAT?
THIS!
HIS FONTANEL?
HAS THAT ALWAYS BEEN THERE!?

BABY
INVENTIONS

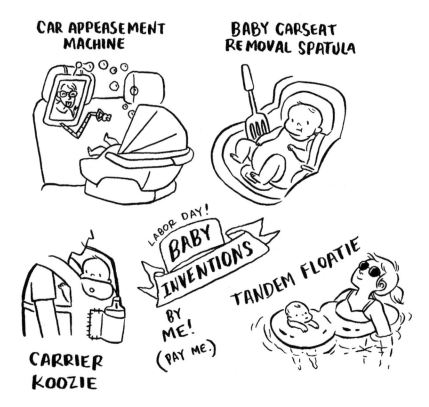

CAR APPEASEMENT MACHINE

BABY CARSEAT REMOVAL SPATULA

CARRIER KOOZIE

LABOR DAY! BABY INVENTIONS BY ME! (PAY ME.)

TANDEM FLOATIE

YET MORE
BABY INVENTIONS
BY ME.

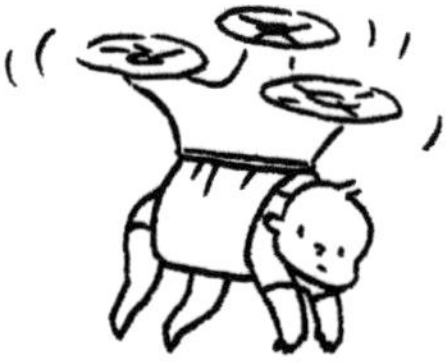

BABY DRONE: FLOATS CRANKY BABY AROUND DINNER TABLE

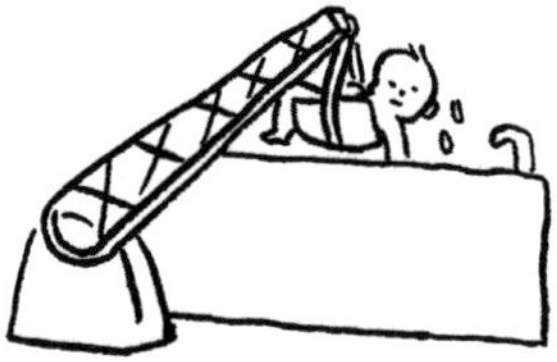

BABY BATH CRANE: WITH SLIP-PROOF GRABBER

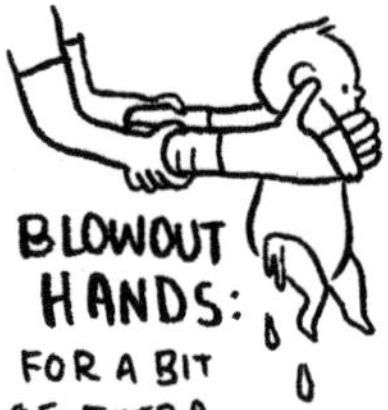

BLOWOUT HANDS: FOR A BIT OF EXTRA DISTANCE

SWINGY
HAPPY LAMP

SOFT
PHOTO
OF PARENTS

MIRROR
W/ KEYBOARD
THAT PLAYS
A TUNE

SOFT PLANT

FLIPPY
BOOK

CRINKLY
PAPERS

BABY DESK!

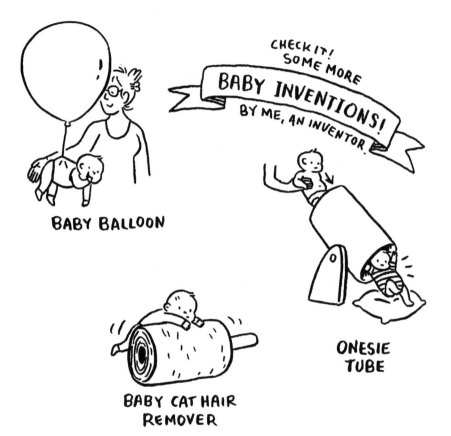

BABY BALLOON

CHECK IT!
SOME MORE
BABY INVENTIONS!
BY ME, AN INVENTOR.

ONESIE
TUBE

BABY CAT HAIR
REMOVER

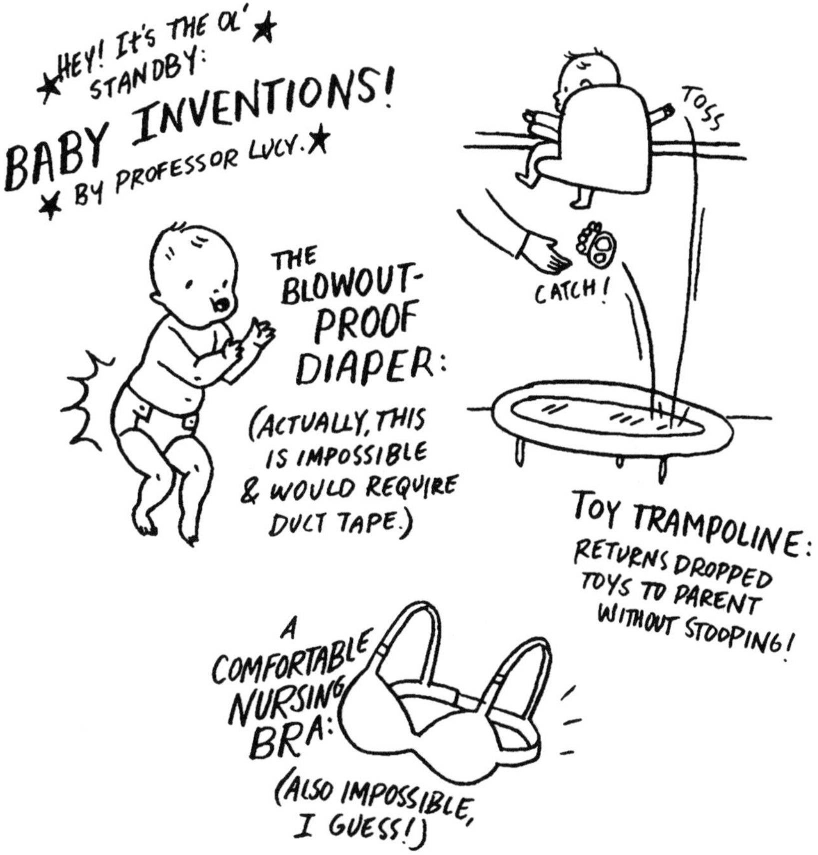
★HEY! IT'S THE OL'★ STANDBY:
BABY INVENTIONS!
★BY PROFESSOR LUCY.★
THE BLOWOUT-PROOF DIAPER:
(ACTUALLY, THIS IS IMPOSSIBLE & WOULD REQUIRE DUCT TAPE.)
TOSS
CATCH!
TOY TRAMPOLINE:
RETURNS DROPPED TOYS TO PARENT WITHOUT STOOPING!
A COMFORTABLE NURSING BRA:
(ALSO IMPOSSIBLE, I GUESS!)

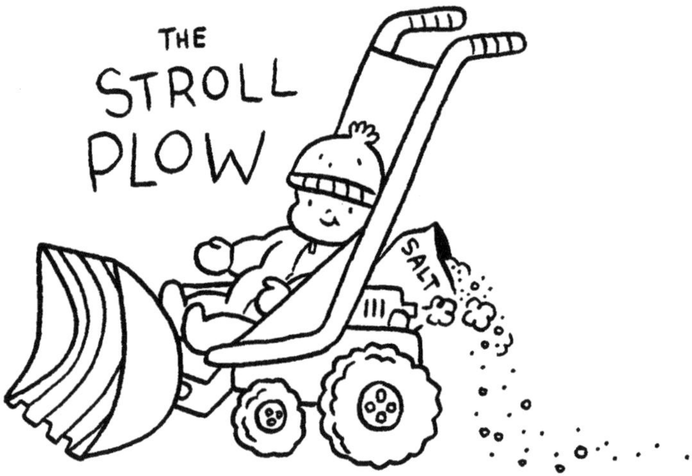
THE
STROLL
PLOW
SALT

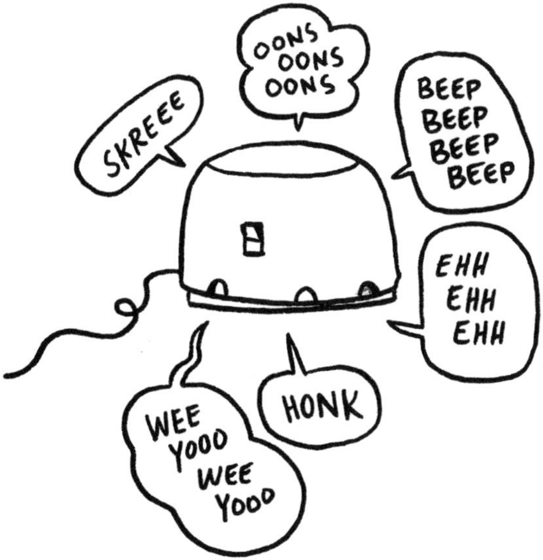
SKREEE
OONS OONS OONS
BEEP BEEP BEEP BEEP
EHH EHH EHH
HONK
WEE YOOO WEE YOOO

THEY SHOULD MAKE A TRAVEL SOUND MACHINE FOR CITY BABIES.

FASHION

THIS HAT IS SO CUTE...

IT HAS STOPPED TRAFFIC.

WHY IS THE SLEEP SACK SOOO LOOONG?

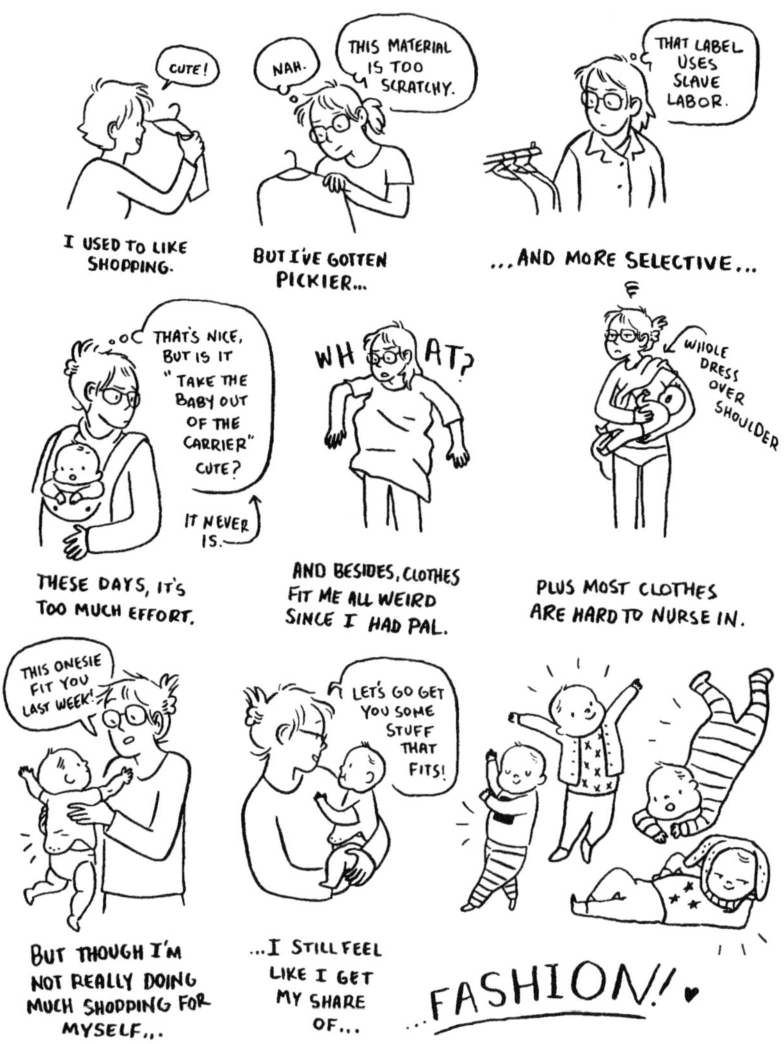

CUTE!
I USED TO LIKE SHOPPING.
NAH.
THIS MATERIAL IS TOO SCRATCHY.
BUT I'VE GOTTEN PICKIER...
THAT LABEL USES SLAVE LABOR.
...AND MORE SELECTIVE...
THAT'S NICE, BUT IS IT "TAKE THE BABY OUT OF THE CARRIER" CUTE?
IT NEVER IS.
THESE DAYS, IT'S TOO MUCH EFFORT.
WH AT?
AND BESIDES, CLOTHES FIT ME ALL WEIRD SINCE I HAD PAL.
WHOLE DRESS OVER SHOULDER
PLUS MOST CLOTHES ARE HARD TO NURSE IN.
THIS ONESIE FIT YOU LAST WEEK!
BUT THOUGH I'M NOT REALLY DOING MUCH SHOPPING FOR MYSELF...
LET'S GO GET YOU SOME STUFF THAT FITS!
...I STILL FEEL LIKE I GET MY SHARE OF...
...FASHION!

NOTHIN'
LIKE
FEELIN'
CUTE
TO
ENSURE
YOU WILL
GET
PUKED,
POOPED
& PEED ON
BY THE END
OF THE DAY.

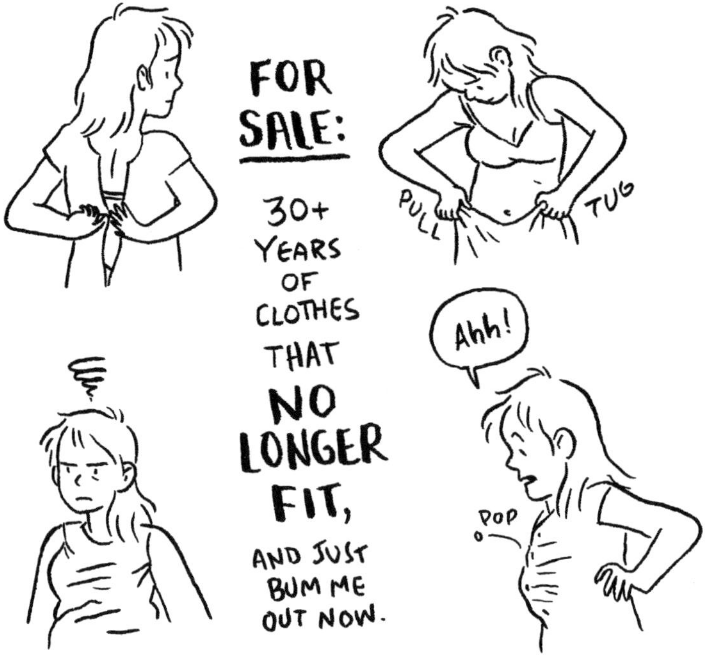
FOR SALE:
30+ YEARS OF CLOTHES THAT NO LONGER FIT, AND JUST BUM ME OUT NOW.
PULL
TUG
Ahh!
POP

TURNS OUT, THE BABY IS...

A HAT PERSON.

BEAUX CHAPEAUX

ANIMAL EARS MAKE HATS EXTRA WARM!

PAL, DO YOU HAVE ENOUGH HAIR FOR ME TO BRUSH IT INTO A COOL MO-HAWK?!
BRUSH
BRUSH
KEWPIE DOLL
YES.
VERY PUNK ROCK.

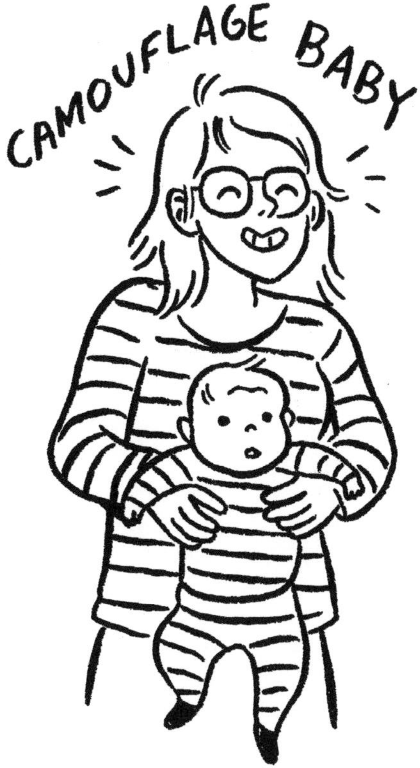
CAMOUFLAGE BABY

The most HILARIOUS BABY SLEEP AID

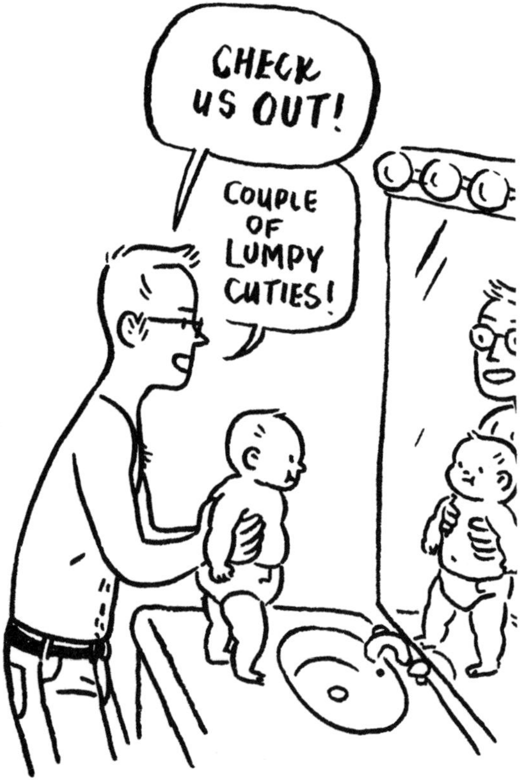
CHECK US OUT!
COUPLE OF LUMPY CUTIES!

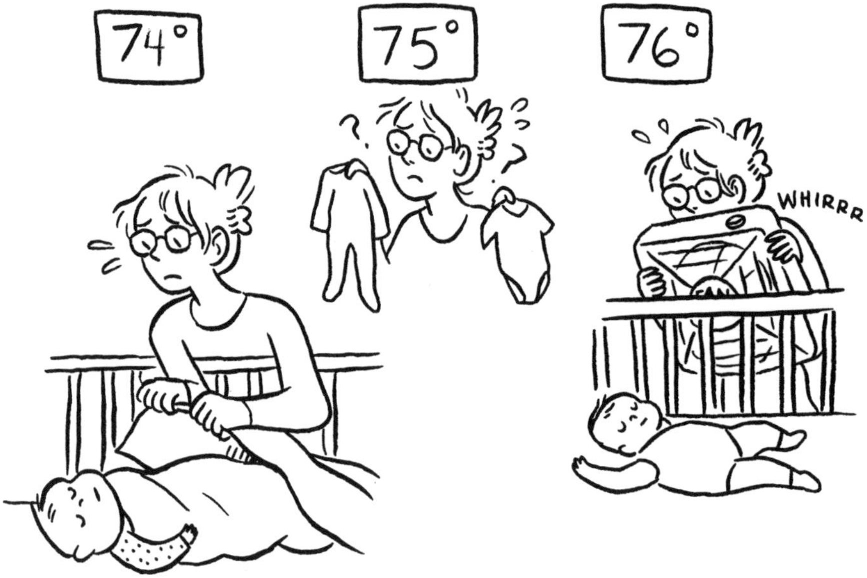
74°
75°
76°
WHIRRR

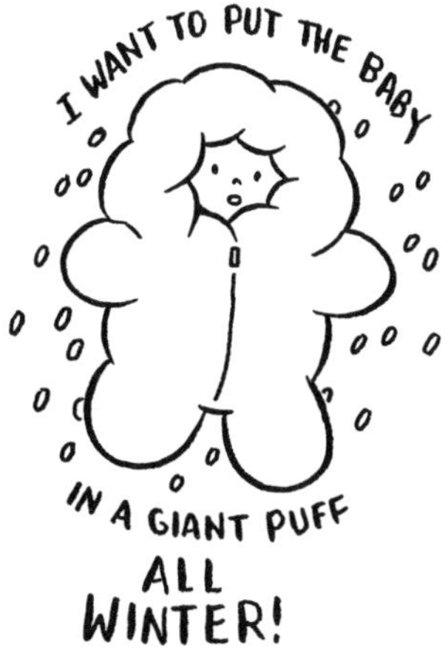
I WANT TO PUT THE BABY
IN A GIANT PUFF
ALL WINTER!

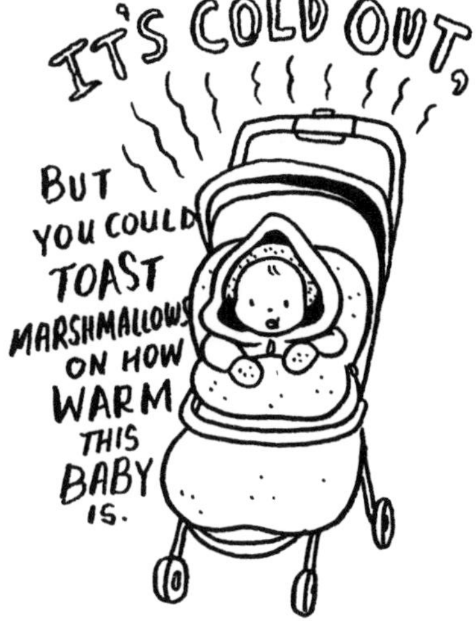
IT'S COLD OUT,
BUT YOU COULD TOAST MARSHMALLOWS ON HOW WARM THIS BABY IS.

Too Hot for BABYWEARING

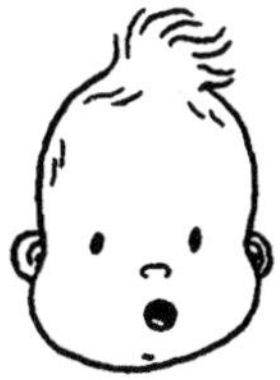

FRESH FROM THE TUBBY PUNK

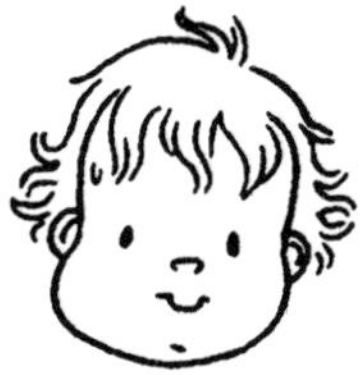

HUMID WEATHER Frasier Crane

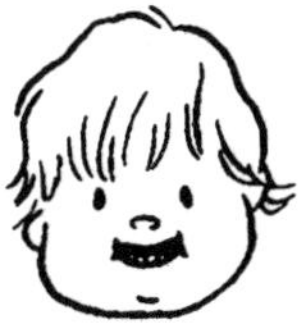

WINDY CAR RIDE TOMMY BOY

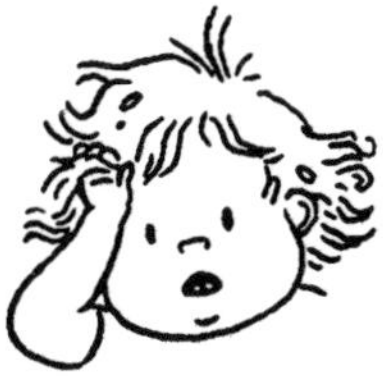

POST-DINNER YOUNG FRANKENSTEIN

BABY HALLOWEEN COSTUMES

THAT WE'RE NOT GONNA USE, BUT I STILL LIKE THEM, SO I'M GONNA DRAW 'EM!

KYLO REN

(WE WOULD BE LEIA & HAN)

I WAS EXCITED TO DRAW EYEBROWS ON THE BABY, BUT THE WIG IS TOO IMPRACTICAL.

TOBY

(FROM LABYRINTH)

I TALKED JOHN INTO BEING JARETH, BUT I WOULDN'T BE ABLE TO GET THE SARAH COSTUME RIGHT ENOUGH TO BE RECOGNIZABLE.

NATHAN JR.

(FROM RAISING ARIZONA)

RELUCTANTLY I WILL ADMIT THAT THIS REFERENCE IS PRETTY DATED.

ALFRED HITCHCOCK

HILARIOUS, BUT HARD TO NOT JUST APPEAR AS "FORMAL BABY"

TOMMY BOY

BUT THEN JOHN WOULD GET TO BE RICHARD & I'D HAVE TO BE LIKE RAY ZALINSKY, WHICH IS GETTING PRETTY OBSCURE.

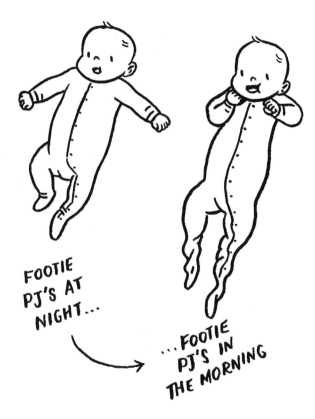

FOOTIE
PJ'S AT
NIGHT...

...FOOTIE
PJ'S IN
THE MORNING

FITS
PERFECTLY

YEP,
THIS IS HOW IT'S
SUPPOSED
TO FIT.

LONG DAYS

RUNNING ON
SNIFF
(BABY)
FUMES

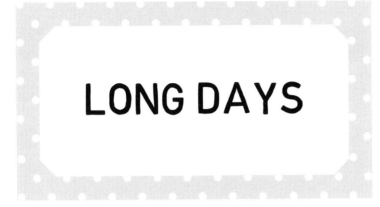

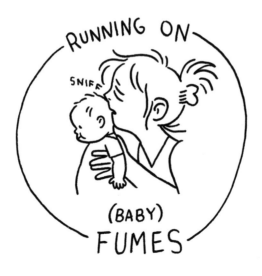

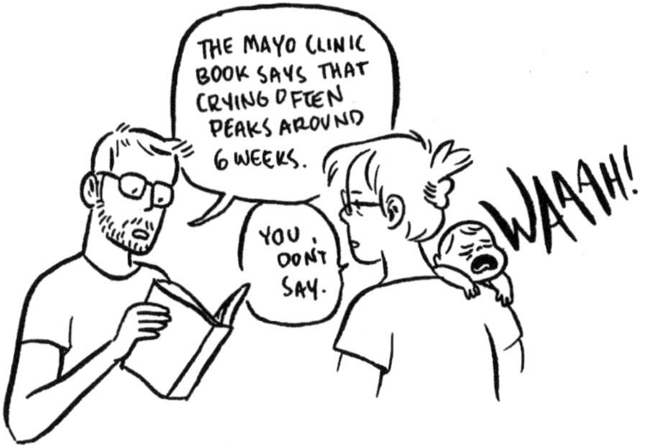
THE MAYO CLINIC BOOK SAYS THAT CRYING OFTEN PEAKS AROUND 6 WEEKS.
YOU DON'T SAY.
WAAAH!

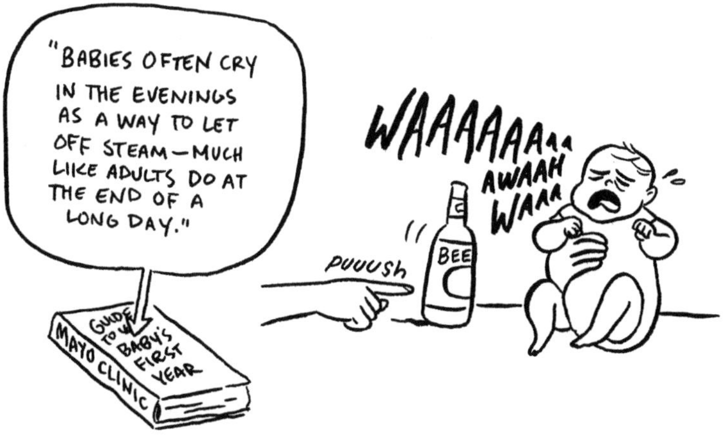
"BABIES OFTEN CRY IN THE EVENINGS AS A WAY TO LET OFF STEAM—MUCH LIKE ADULTS DO AT THE END OF A LONG DAY."
GUIDE TO YOUR BABY'S FIRST YEAR
MAYO CLINIC
WAAAAAAaaa
AWAAH
WAAA
PUUUSH
BEE

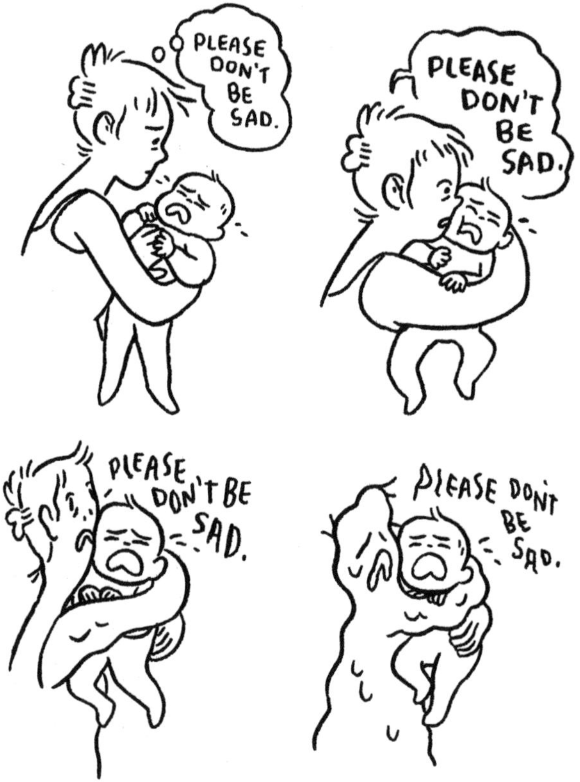
PLEASE DON'T BE SAD.
PLEASE DON'T BE SAD.
PLEASE DON'T BE SAD.
PLEASE DON'T BE SAD.

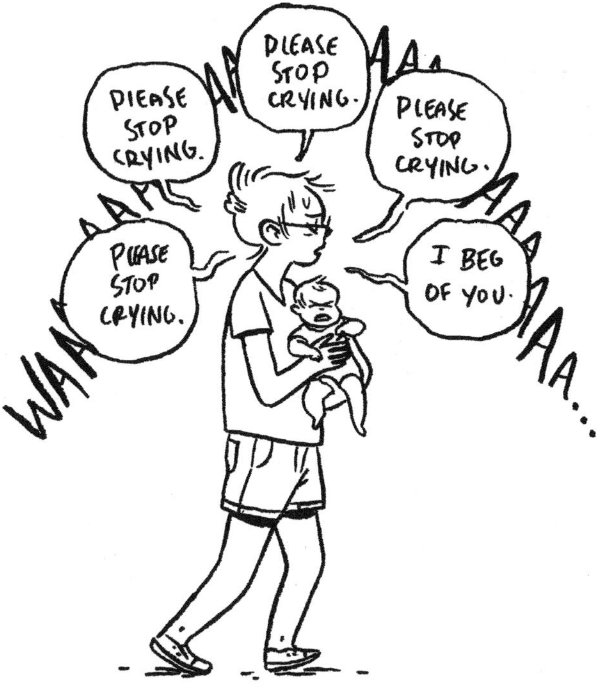
WAAAAAAAAAAAAAAAA...
PLEASE STOP CRYING.
PLEASE STOP CRYING.
PLEASE STOP CRYING.
PLEASE STOP CRYING.
I BEG OF YOU.

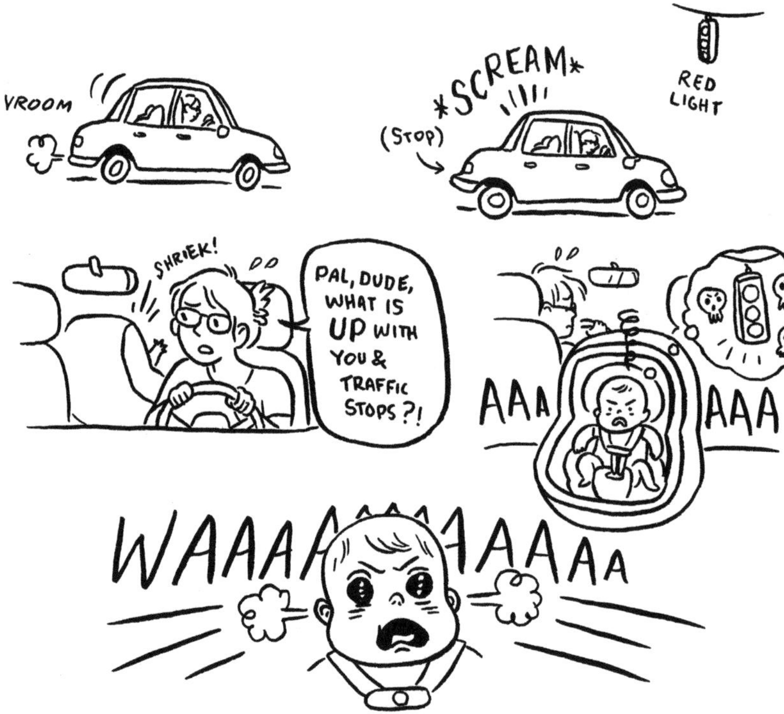
VROOM
SCREAM
(STOP)
RED LIGHT
SHRIEK!
PAL, DUDE, WHAT IS UP WITH YOU & TRAFFIC STOPS?!
AAA
AAA
WAAAAAAAAAAAA

Pal
 ⭐1 📷0

☆★★★★

This hotel is **NOT** my house! It smells all wrong and is totally unfamiliar to me. I don't know how anyone can be expected to sleep under these conditions. Did enjoy the stripey curtains, tho.

THE BABY'S HEAD

GETS
SQUARE
WHEN HE'S UPSET.

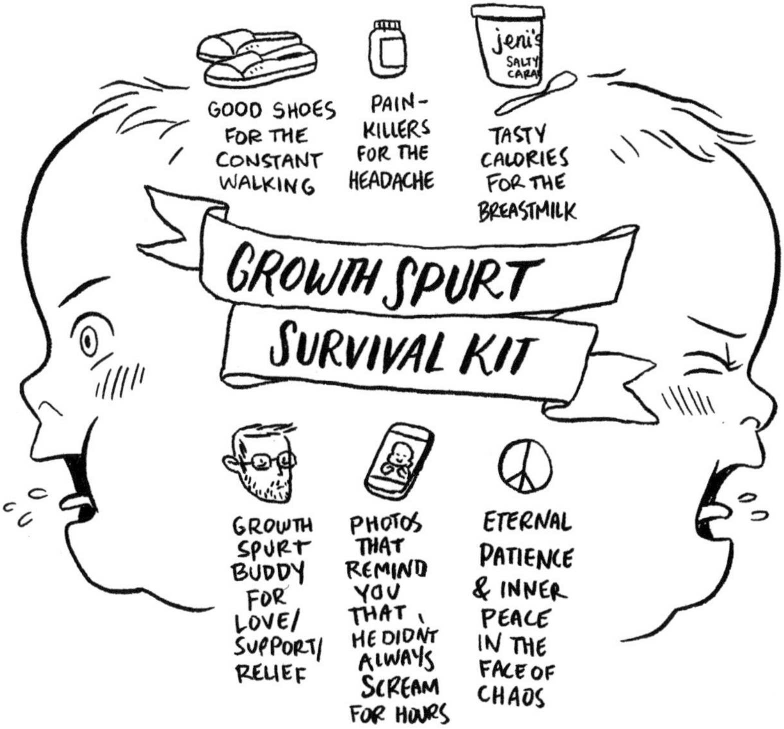
jeni's
SALTY CARA
GOOD SHOES FOR THE CONSTANT WALKING
PAIN-KILLERS FOR THE HEADACHE
TASTY CALORIES FOR THE BREASTMILK
GROWTH SPURT SURVIVAL KIT
GROWTH SPURT BUDDY FOR LOVE/ SUPPORT/ RELIEF
PHOTOS THAT REMIND YOU THAT HE DIDN'T ALWAYS SCREAM FOR HOURS
ETERNAL PATIENCE & INNER PEACE IN THE FACE OF CHAOS

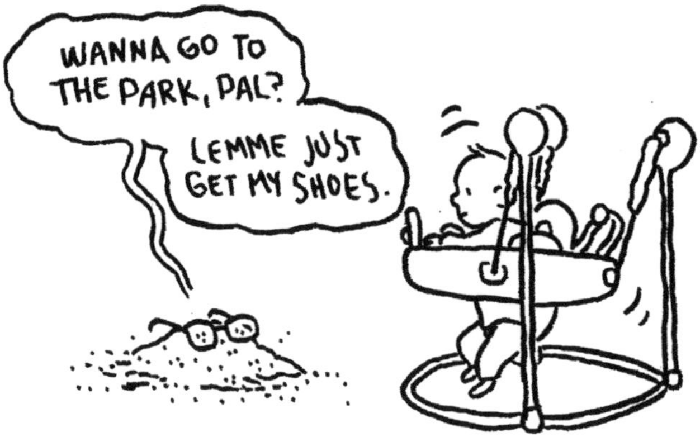
WANNA GO TO THE PARK, PAL?
LEMME JUST GET MY SHOES.

I'm sorry, sweetie. I know it hurts.

EHHH!

I've officially decided that I think the baby is teething, even though he's only fifteen weeks.

EHH!

FLAIL

SWIPE

THE trouble with this is that he can't really hold a teether, yet.

HAIR

DIRT

LINT

His little hands are always cold & wet. AND STICKY.

CRAM

STUFF

EAT

NO WONDER.

I WANT to always have perfect patience & serenity welling from my sympathy for him, but...

90 MINUTES OF THIS

HASN'T EATEN

GO. TO. SLEEP!

PUT US BOTH OUT OF OUR MISERY!

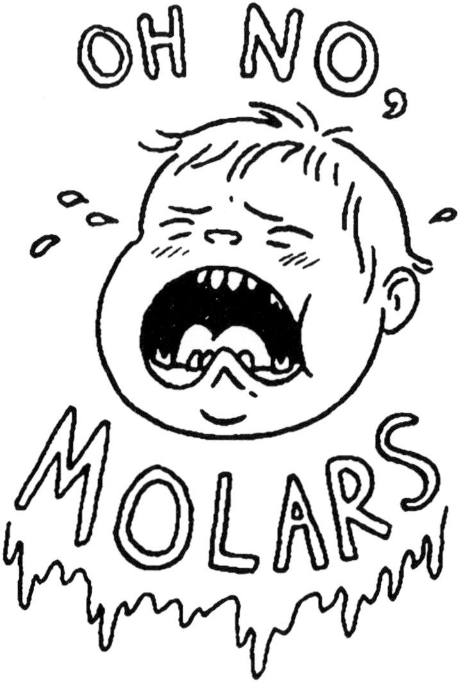
OH NO,
MOLARS

WANTED

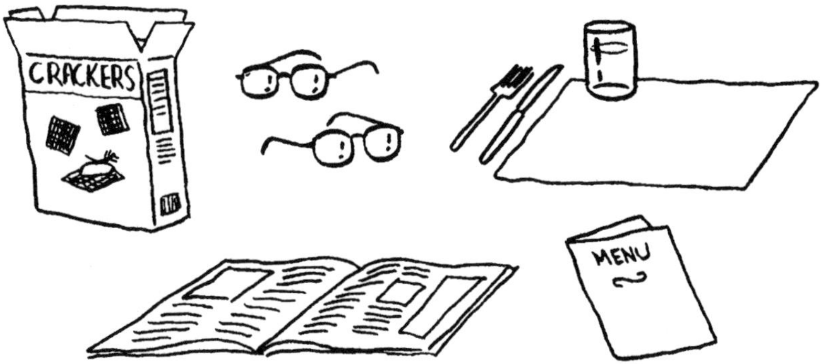
CRACKERS
MENU

IF YOU SEE THESE ITEMS, GRAB THEM! PUT THEM IMMEDIATELY INTO YOUR MOUTH!

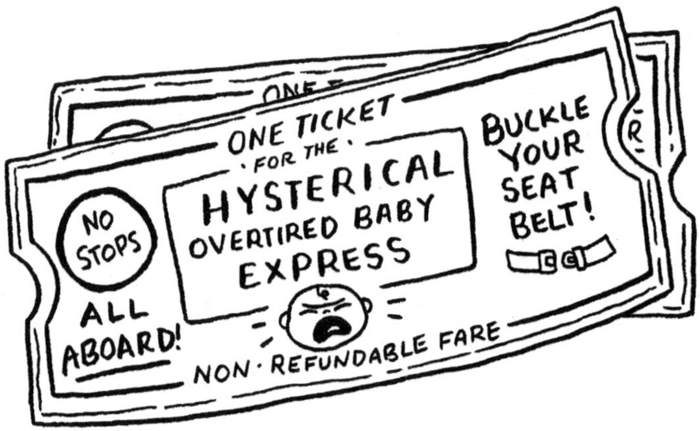
ONE TICKET
FOR THE
HYSTERICAL
OVERTIRED BABY
EXPRESS
NO STOPS
ALL ABOARD!
BUCKLE YOUR SEAT BELT!
NON-REFUNDABLE FARE

AN INTERNATIONAL FLIGHT...
A BABY...
A MESSY DIAPER...
& VERY GOOD DADDING!

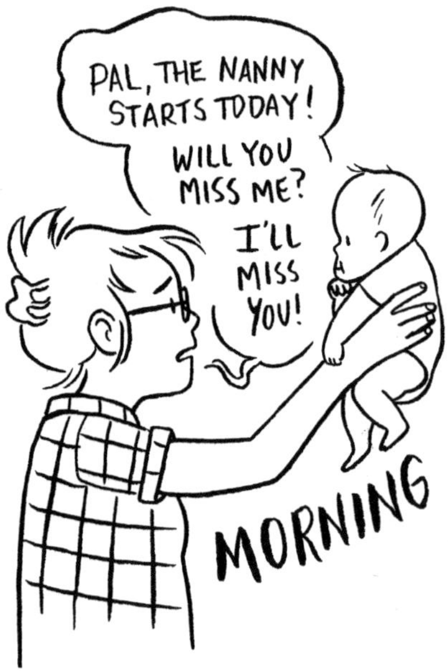
PAL, THE NANNY STARTS TODAY!
WILL YOU MISS ME?
I'LL MISS YOU!
MORNING

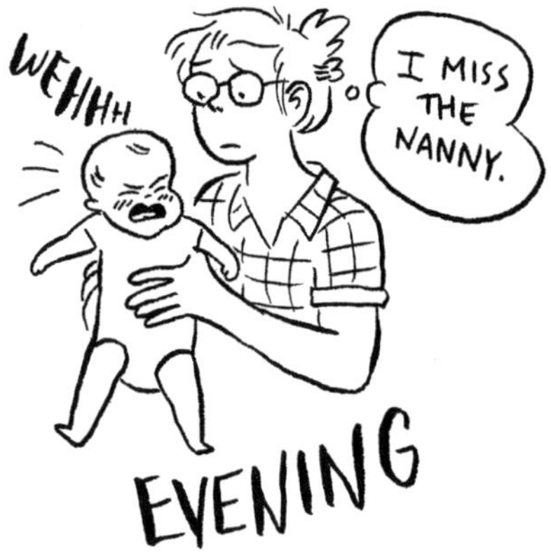
WEHHHH
I MISS THE NANNY.
EVENING

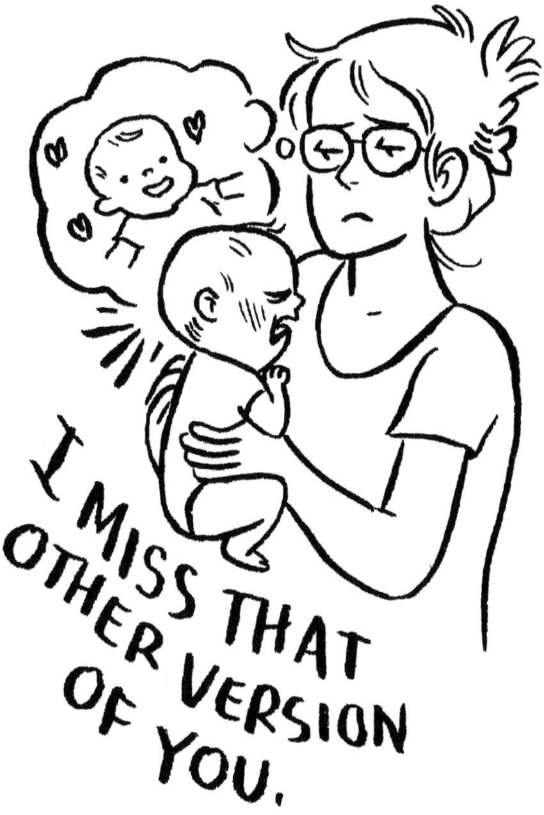
I MISS THAT OTHER VERSION OF YOU.

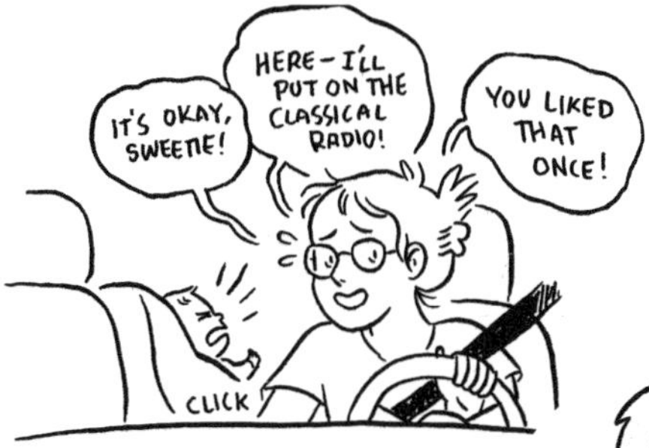
IT'S OKAY, SWEETIE!
HERE—I'LL PUT ON THE CLASSICAL RADIO!
YOU LIKED THAT ONCE!
CLICK

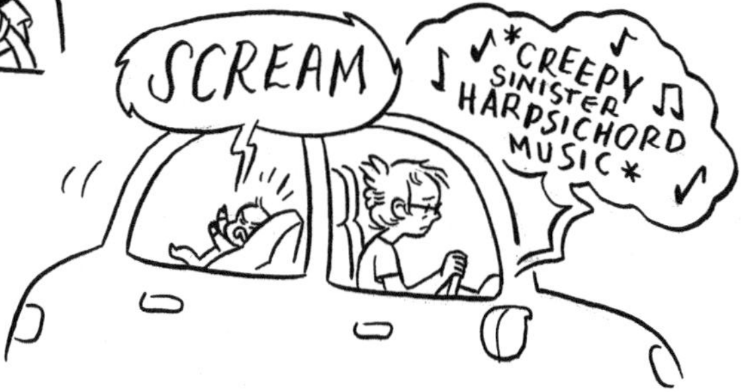
SCREAM
CREEPY SINISTER HARPSICHORD MUSIC

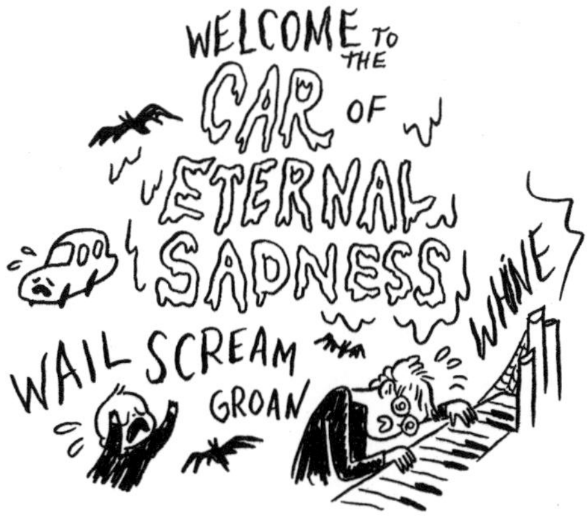
WELCOME TO THE CAR OF ETERNAL SADNESS
WAIL
SCREAM
GROAN
WHINE

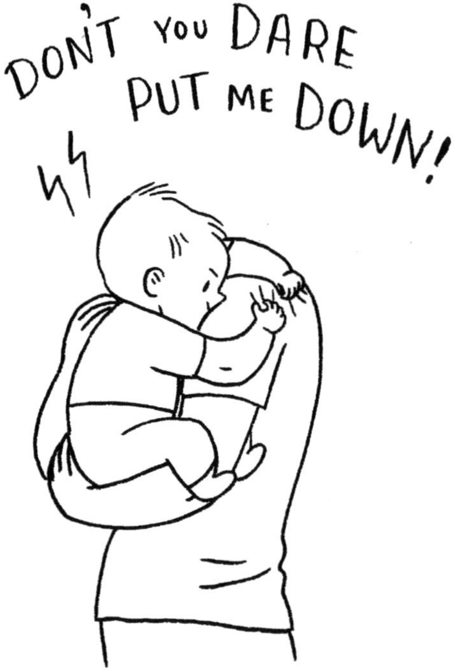
DON'T YOU DARE
PUT ME DOWN!

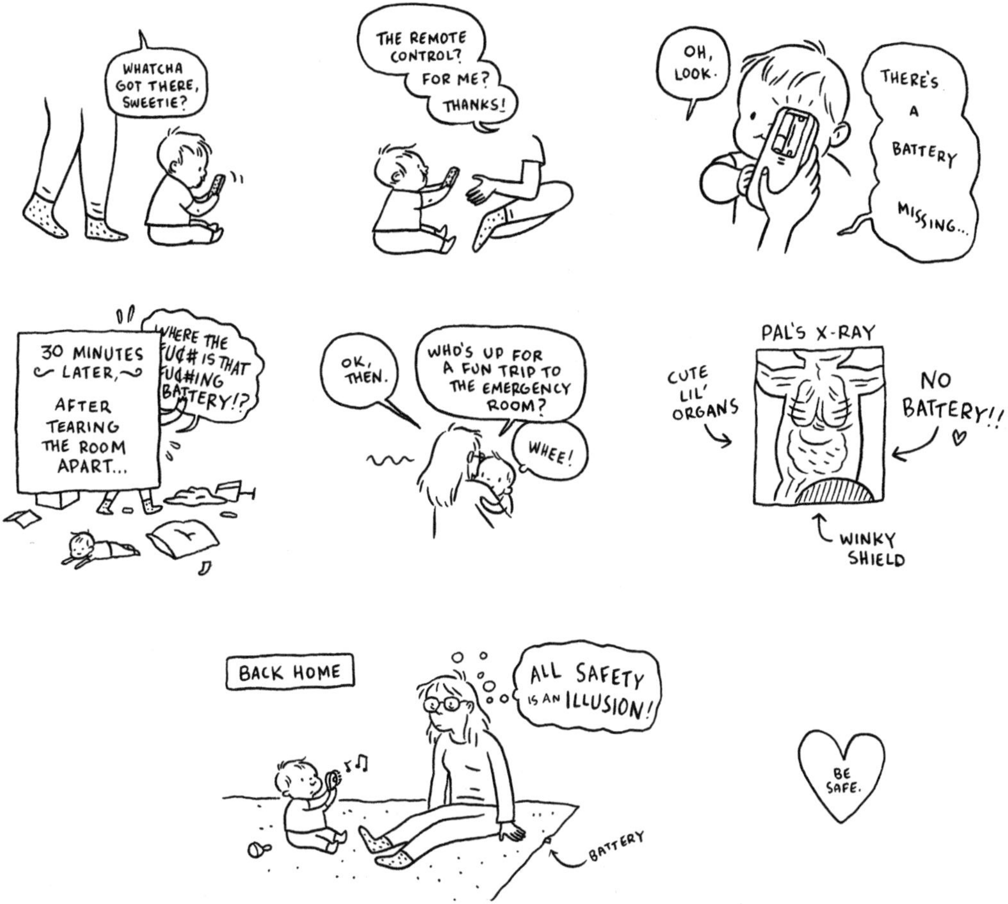
WHATCHA GOT THERE, SWEETIE?
THE REMOTE CONTROL?
FOR ME?
THANKS!
OH, LOOK.
THERE'S A BATTERY MISSING...
30 MINUTES LATER,
AFTER TEARING THE ROOM APART...
WHERE THE FUC# IS THAT FUC#ING BATTERY!?
OK, THEN.
WHO'S UP FOR A FUN TRIP TO THE EMERGENCY ROOM?
WHEE!
PAL'S X-RAY
CUTE LIL' ORGANS
NO BATTERY!!
WINKY SHIELD
BACK HOME
ALL SAFETY IS AN ILLUSION!
BATTERY
BE SAFE.

SOME DAYS, it feels like there's Nothing Left.

SLEEPLESSNESS, SCREAMING & TEETHING ARE FLEETING.

SHORT YEARS

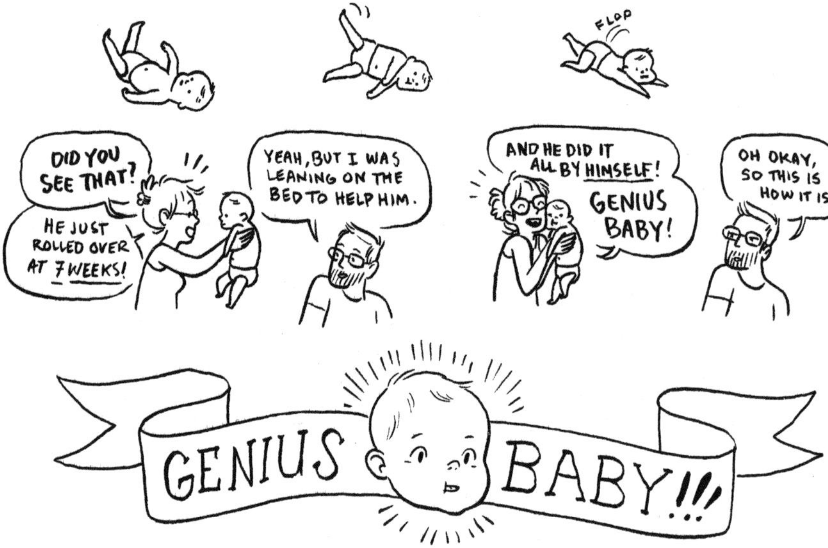
FLOP
DID YOU SEE THAT?
HE JUST ROLLED OVER AT 7 WEEKS!
YEAH, BUT I WAS LEANING ON THE BED TO HELP HIM.
AND HE DID IT ALL BY HIMSELF!
GENIUS BABY!
OH OKAY, SO THIS IS HOW IT IS.
GENIUS BABY!!!

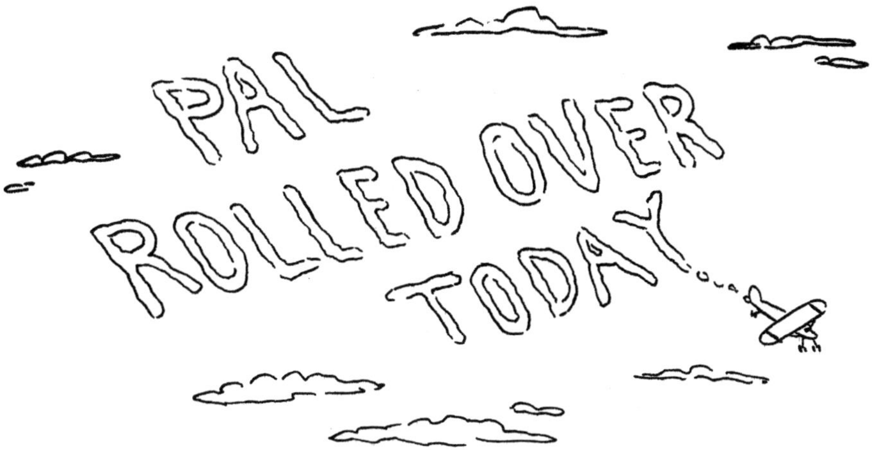
PAL
ROLLED OVER
TODAY

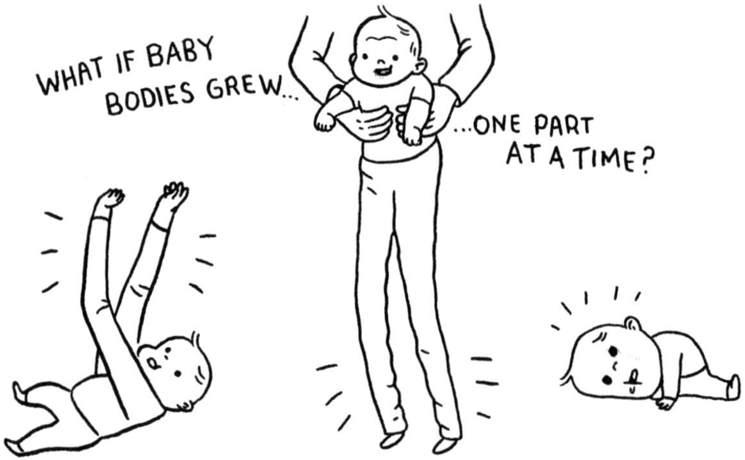
WHAT IF BABY
BODIES GREW...
...ONE PART
AT A TIME?

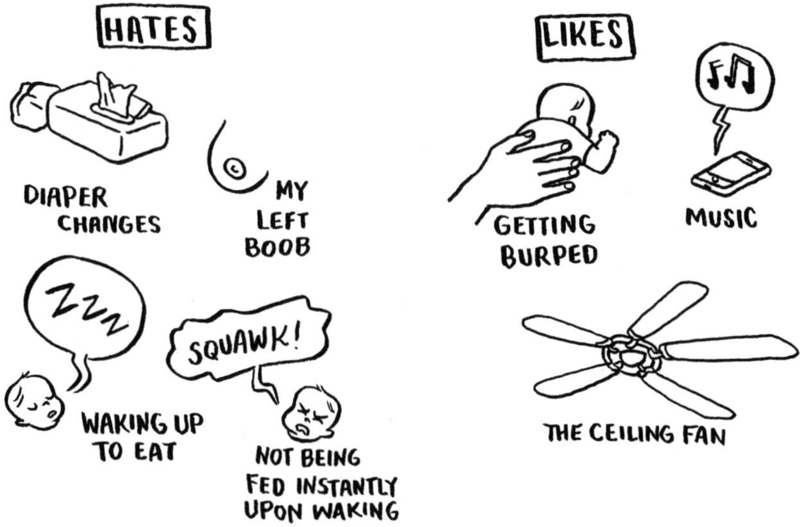
HATES
DIAPER CHANGES
MY LEFT BOOB
ZZZ
WAKING UP TO EAT
SQUAWK!
NOT BEING FED INSTANTLY UPON WAKING
LIKES
GETTING BURPED
MUSIC
THE CEILING FAN

BABY IMPRESSIONS
TREE FROG
EEHHHZZZ
EEHHZZZ
ANGRY BEE
WINDMILL
THRASH THRASH
SNORT SNORT SNORT
PIGGY

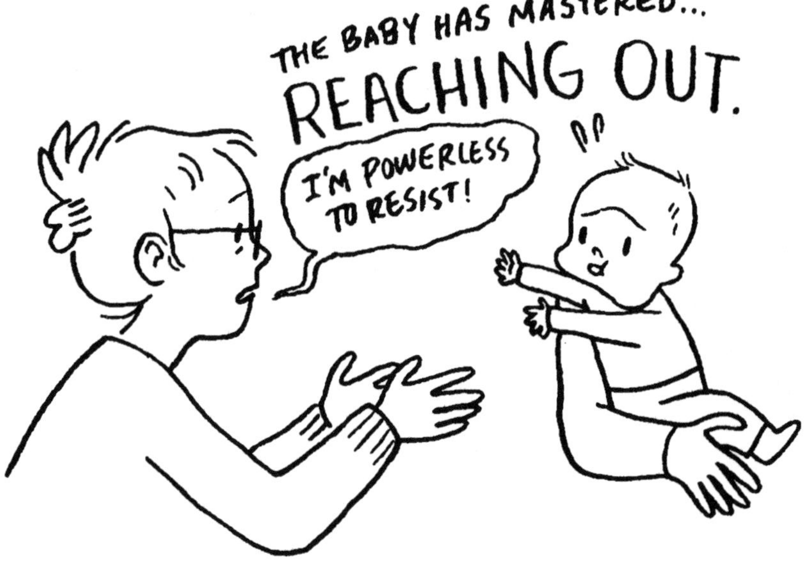
THE BABY HAS MASTERED...
REACHING OUT.
I'M POWERLESS TO RESIST!

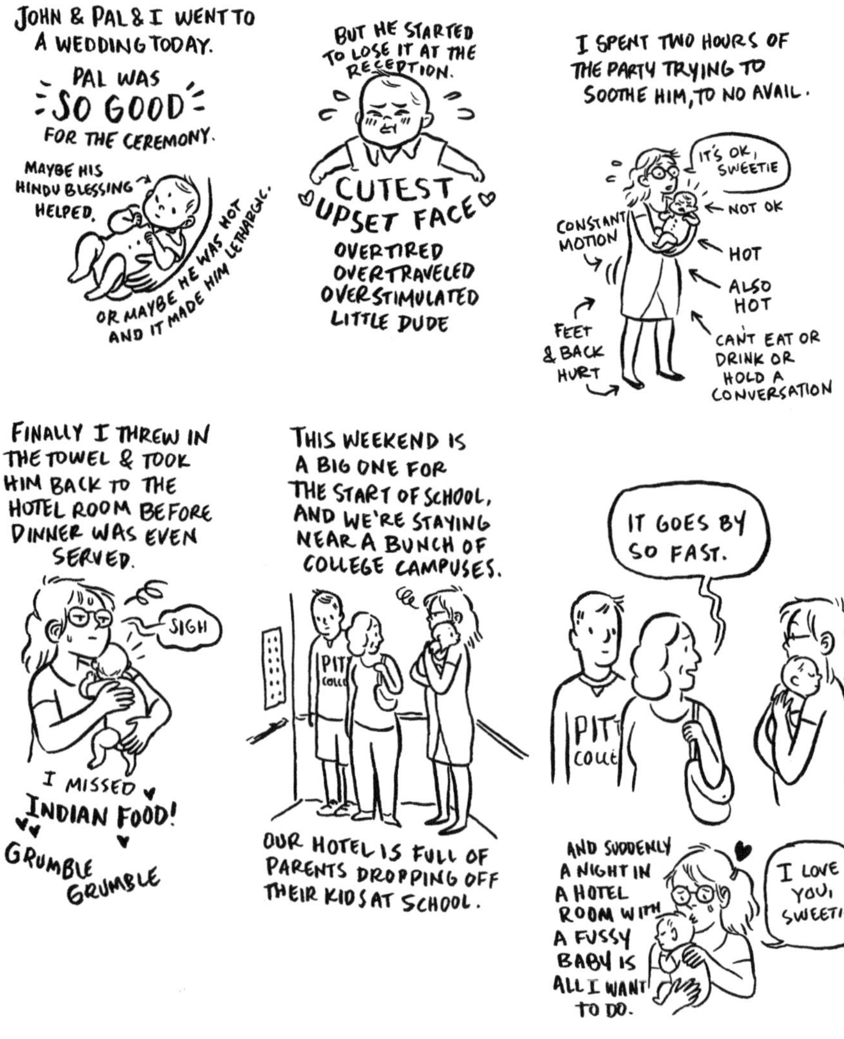
JOHN & PAL & I WENT TO A WEDDING TODAY.
PAL WAS SO GOOD FOR THE CEREMONY.
MAYBE HIS HINDU BLESSING HELPED.
OR MAYBE HE WAS HOT AND IT MADE HIM LETHARGIC.
BUT HE STARTED TO LOSE IT AT THE RECEPTION.
CUTEST UPSET FACE
OVERTIRED OVERTRAVELED OVERSTIMULATED LITTLE DUDE
I SPENT TWO HOURS OF THE PARTY TRYING TO SOOTHE HIM, TO NO AVAIL.
IT'S OK, SWEETIE
NOT OK
CONSTANT MOTION
HOT
ALSO HOT
FEET & BACK HURT
CAN'T EAT OR DRINK OR HOLD A CONVERSATION
FINALLY I THREW IN THE TOWEL & TOOK HIM BACK TO THE HOTEL ROOM BEFORE DINNER WAS EVEN SERVED.
SIGH
I MISSED INDIAN FOOD!
GRUMBLE GRUMBLE
THIS WEEKEND IS A BIG ONE FOR THE START OF SCHOOL, AND WE'RE STAYING NEAR A BUNCH OF COLLEGE CAMPUSES.
OUR HOTEL IS FULL OF PARENTS DROPPING OFF THEIR KIDS AT SCHOOL.
IT GOES BY SO FAST.
AND SUDDENLY A NIGHT IN A HOTEL ROOM WITH A FUSSY BABY IS ALL I WANT TO DO.
I LOVE YOU, SWEETIE.

THE CAR MIRROR
DISTORTS PAL'S
REFLECTION AT
THE EDGES IN A
HILARIOUS WAY.

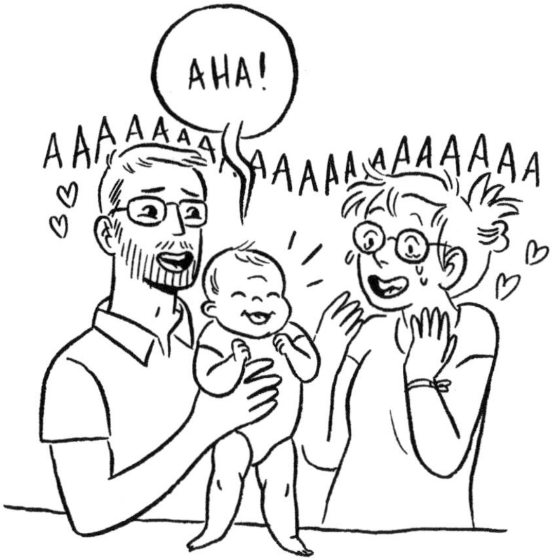
AHA!
AAAAAAAA
AAAAAAAAAAAAA

The baby has just begun
to Laugh,
and it is...
The Best.

WE'VE ENTERED

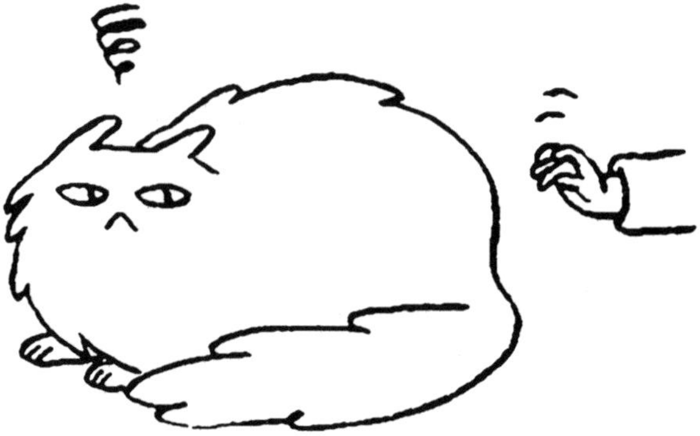

A NEW PHASE
of
GRABBINESS

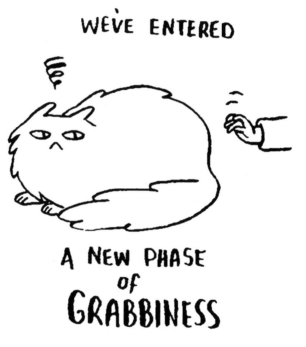

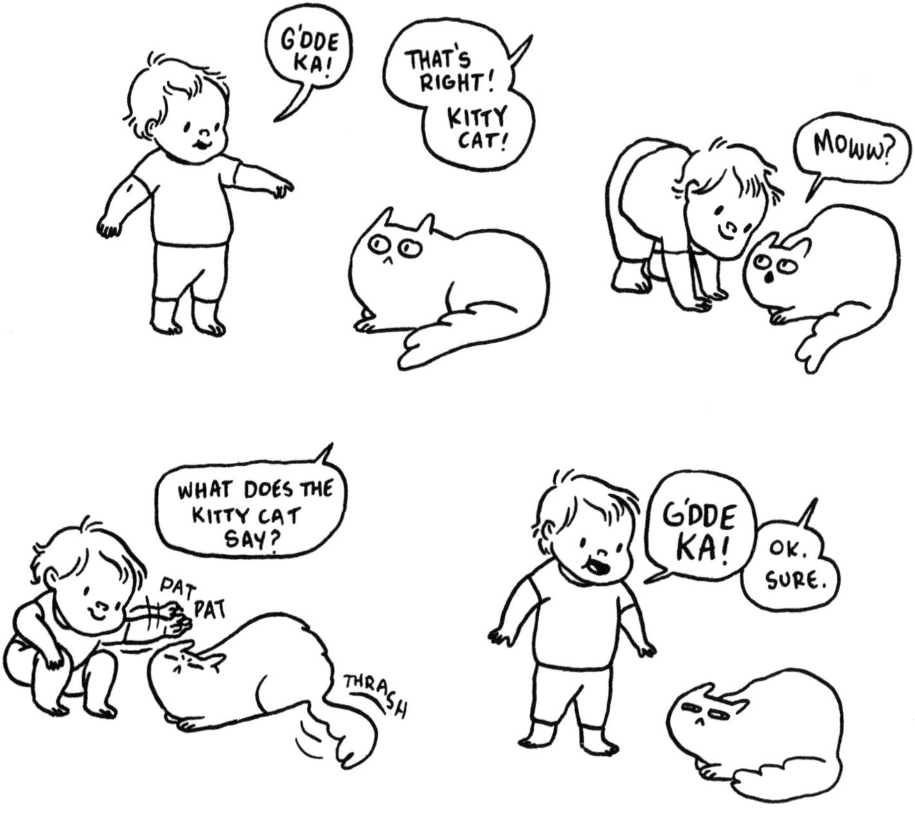

G'DDE KA!
THAT'S RIGHT!
KITTY CAT!
MOWW?
WHAT DOES THE KITTY CAT SAY?
PAT PAT
THRASH
G'DDE KA!
OK. SURE.

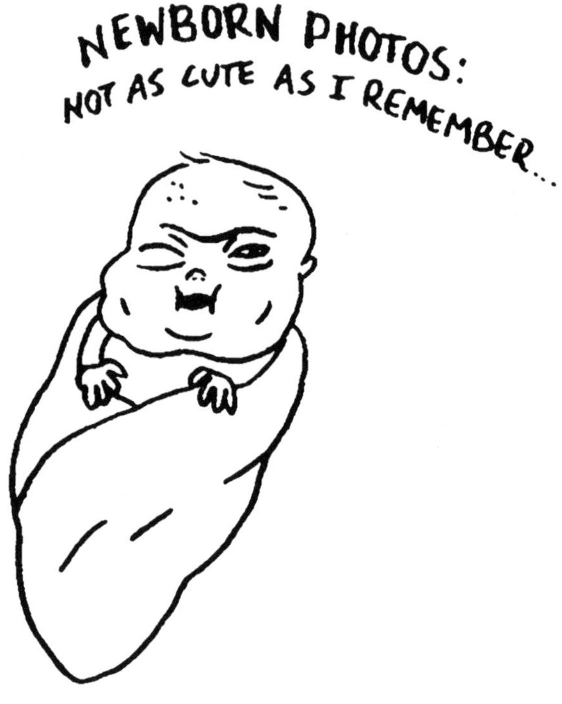
NEWBORN PHOTOS:
NOT AS CUTE AS I REMEMBER...

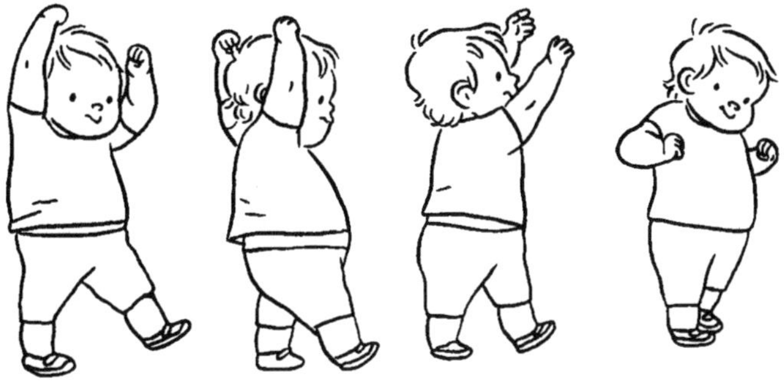

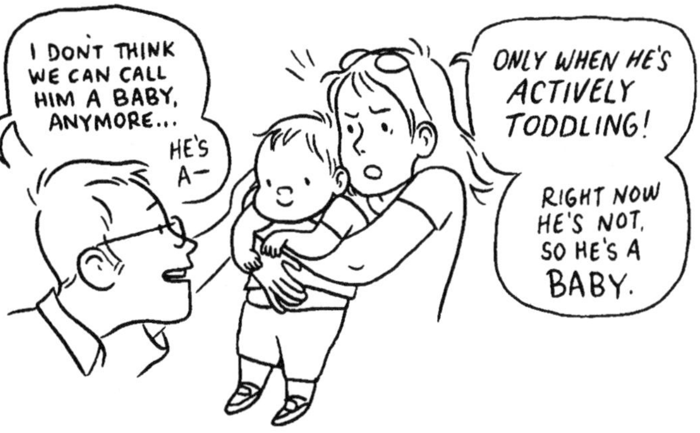
I DON'T THINK WE CAN CALL HIM A BABY, ANYMORE...
HE'S A—
ONLY WHEN HE'S ACTIVELY TODDLING!
RIGHT NOW HE'S NOT, SO HE'S A BABY.

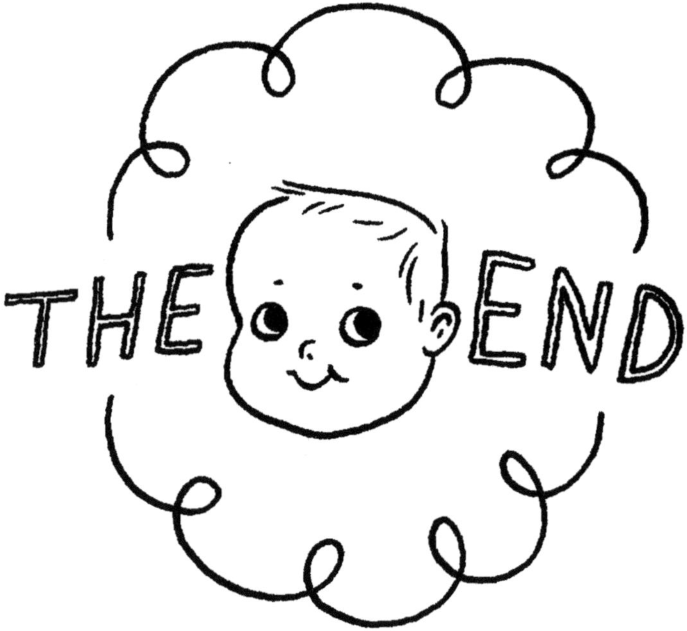
THE END

Thank you Holly, Kiara, Angelika, John, and all of Pal's grands.

And to anyone who has ever seen a screaming baby with their parent in public and expressed sympathy and kindness.

LUCY KNISLEY is a bestselling author and artist of graphic novels and children's books. She lives in Chicago, where she spends a lot of time drawing and writing her stories from the enormous toy pile that used to be her office. She previously published the *New York Times* bestseller *Relish: My Life in the Kitchen*, *Something New: Tales from a Makeshift Bride*, and *Kid Gloves* with First Second.

lucyknisley.com

First Second

Published by First Second
First Second is an imprint of Roaring Brook Press, a division
of Holtzbrinck Publishing Holdings Limited Partnership
120 Broadway, New York, NY 10271

Don't miss your next favorite book from First Second! For the latest updates
go to firstsecondnewsletter.com and sign up for our enewsletter.

Library of Congress Control Number: 2019930665
ISBN: 978-1-250-21149-1

Our books may be purchased in bulk for promotional, educational, or business use.
Please contact your local bookseller or the Macmillan Corporate and Premium Sales Department
at (800) 221-7945 ext. 5442 or by email at MacmillanSpecialMarkets@macmillan.com.

First edition, 2020
Edited by Calista Brill and Kiara Valdez
Book design by Andrew Arnold and Eileen Savage
Printed in China

Straight to ink with a Kuretake ZIG Letter Pen on cheap bristol in a homemade sketchbook, often smudged by breastmilk.

1 3 5 7 9 10 8 6 4 2